Navy Pier: *A Chicago Landmark*

Navy Pier

A Chicago Landmark

Douglas Bukowski

© Metropolitan Pier and Exposition Authority 1996

Published by

Metropolitan Pier and Exposition Authority
2301 S. Prairie Avenue
Chicago, Illinois 60616

All photographs without specific credit lines are
used courtesy of the Chicago Historical Society.

Cover photo by Vito Palmisano

Distributed by

Ivan R. Dee, Inc.
Publisher
1332 North Halsted Street
Chicago, Illinois 60622-2637
Fax: 312-787-6269
Phone: 312-787-6262

Library of Congress Cataloging-in-Publication Data

Bukowski, Douglas, 1952–
    Navy Pier : a Chicago landmark / Douglas Bukowski.
        p.   cm.
    Includes bibliographical references.
    ISBN: 978-1-56663-115-0 ISBN 1-56663-115-7 (paperback)
    1. Navy Pier (Chicago, Ill.)—History.   2. Navy Pier (Chicago,
Ill.)—History—Pictorial works.   3. Chicago (Ill.)—Buildings,
structures, etc.   4. Chicago (Ill.)—Buildings, structures, etc.—
Pictorial works.   I. Title.
F548.63.N38B85   1996
725'.8042'0977311—dc20   96-7710
                                                                  CIP

Contents

Preface

City landmarks are precious things. All too often, events conspire to take from us places filled with memory and history: the ballpark of Appling and Veeck, the movie house where we watched enviously as Charlton Heston drove his chariot, the amusement park that promised it would make us laugh our troubles away. When these places vanish, we lose part of ourselves; we also lose a connection to those who came before us and to those who will follow. These are the times when the price of progress becomes too expensive.

Since its opening in 1916, Navy Pier has been every bit a landmark. As a youngster in the 1920s, my father traveled to the pier so he could board a steamer, the *S.S. Carolina*, that would take him to Boy Scout camp across Lake Michigan. In the 1950s, I attended trade fairs at the pier. I do not recall meeting Queen Elizabeth or Prince Philip, but I distinctly remember the toy ambulance my mother bought for me; it was a Chevrolet. I also remember the ships sent by the navy, as far and many as my small eyes could see.

My sister was one of the 100,000 students who would attend the University of Illinois at Navy Pier. She took me with her one evening, and I was able to see what she did every school day. The hallways were incredibly long (and, I learned later, the time between classes far too short). But she seemed to enjoy the experience.

Together with many other Chicagoans, I rediscovered the pier during the Bicentennial in 1976. I came to see the tall ship *Christian Radich* and stayed for the scenery. It was incomprehensible to me that the pier should have fallen into disuse. Like city architect Jerome Butler, who did so much then and more recently to restore the pier, I realized that a grand ballroom on the lakefront is not a resource to be wasted.

I now take my family to the rebuilt Navy Pier. My daughter can see where her grandfather left for camp and her aunt scurried to class; all the family memories are there as the pier readies itself to create more.

This book offers the public story of Navy Pier—its roots in the Chicago Plan and the city's attempt to become a world port; its use by Big Bill Thompson for his Pageants of Progress; the first Golden Age, when Chicagoans came to stroll and eat and play; and the pier's role as a school both during and after World War II. It also tells the story of the pier's decline as a harbor facility and near demise, its proposed use as the foundation for a space needle, and its dominance of Chicago politics as a development issue. ChicagoFest also receives its due, assuming that words can capture the excitement and crowds of those summer celebrations. Somehow, the pier survived it all.

And now, as Navy Pier closes in on its one hundredth birthday, it will continue to greet visitors into the next century. This is all any landmark could want.

Doug Bukowski

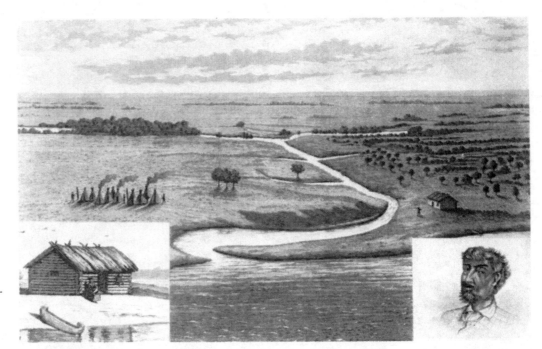

Chicago's first permanent resident was the Haitian emigre Jean Baptiste Point du Sable (*insert*). Like those who followed him, du Sable understood that water transportation would be the key to the region's development.

City Foundations

Chicago is forever changing: The prairie and portage give way to settlement, which in turn becomes a city that seems to insist on reinventing itself every decade. But there is at least one constant throughout the city's history. Chicago's central location makes it a place that allows for the easy movement of people and goods. So the early Native Americans utilized trails and canoes while a later generation of area residents drives the expressways, traffic permitting.

And yet there is more to Chicago than work and exit ramps. This is, after all, where Carl Sandburg found, "The fog comes/ on little cat feet" and "By night the skyscraper looms in the smoke and the stars and has a soul." It is only natural that such a city would choose a design no less beautiful than practical in building a three-thousand-foot long pier for commerce and recreation.

Chicago's first permanent resident sensed the commercial possibilities of an area located at the base of the Great Lakes and within an easy portage of the Mississippi River system. Jean Baptiste Point du Sable, a Haitian emigre, arrived in the 1770s to establish a trading post. Eventually, du Sable erected a complex of nine buildings that stretched a quarter of a mile east and north from the mouth of the Chicago River, to what is now State Street. Du Sable's trading post also served as a center for community. Here Europeans and Indians shared company as they made a living in the place named for the wild onion or skunk grass that flourished along the banks of the river.

Du Sable left the area in 1800. According to some reports, he hoped to become chief of his wife's people, the Pottawatomie. In any event, the founder did not get to witness the growth of the settlement he had begun. Chicago's development continued as the United States government established a formal presence with the construction of a fort in 1803. The installation was named for Secretary of War Henry Dearborn.

As du Sable and the native peoples had earlier, the American government understood that the junction of lake, river and plain created an important transportation hub. Fort Dearborn, located on the south bank of the river across from du Sable's compound, was abandoned during the War of 1812 and rebuilt in 1816. When the garrison pulled out a final time in 1836, Chicago was only two months away from incorporating as a city and already anticipating the benefits of its first great transportation project.

The United States indulged in a peculiar fad the first half of the nineteenth century; it was a kind of "canal craze" that led to 3,326 miles of construction around the country, mostly between 1824 and 1840. People just had to dig, if perhaps for no other reason than to copy the success of De Witt Clinton and the Erie Canal.

Governor of New York in 1817, Clinton dreamed that a canal linking Albany on the Hudson River to Buffalo on Lake Erie would help to create what became the Empire State. Critics decried "Clinton's Big Ditch" and the use of state funds to dig it, but when the canal opened in 1825, doubters were soon proven wrong. The Erie Canal generated so much traffic and revenue that, just ten years after its opening, the state decided to expand it to nearly double in width and depth. Other states, Illinois included, gambled they could repeat New York's success with a canal of their own.

The concept of the Illinois venture actually predated the Erie Canal by some 150 years. His explorations of the Mississippi River Valley in the 1670s left Frenchman Louis Jolliet convinced "we could go with ease to Florida in a bark [boat] and by very easy navigation. It would be necessary to make a canal by cutting through but half a league of prairie, to pass from the foot of Lake Michigan to the Des Plaines [River]."

If Louis XIV could not be bothered with the idea, Secretary of War John C. Calhoun was more accommodating. In 1819 Calhoun included an Illinois canal on his list of transportation projects necessary for national defense. Congress later provided land both for the route and for the state to sell to help fund construction.

Actual work began in 1836. When it was finished twelve years later at a cost of $6.5 million, the ninety-seven-mile-long Illinois and Michigan Canal connected Chicago with the Illinois River at the town of La Salle. The canal was dug by a largely immigrant Irish work force recruited from the East Coast. Laborers endured conditions that verged on wretched: Cholera, malaria and exhaustion from fourteen-to-fifteen-hour workdays netted an average wage of a dollar a day. "You are aware," read one workers' petition, "that from one-half past four in the morning until . . . a quarter of eight in the evening is too long to be withstood at hard labor and by men who have got to stand it in a hot climate in a sickly state and for month after month."

The canal brought trade and, with it, prosperity. Canal boats carried corn up to Chicago, lumber and manufactured goods back down. Trade nurtured the merchants, bankers and shippers who would form the city's commercial foundation. The canal had at least one other effect. A bridge over the canal at its Chicago terminus gave a name to the surrounding neighborhood, where many of the construction workers had settled. The area first called Hardscrabble, in reference either to the soil or the inhabitants, would become known as Bridgeport.

The canal came to Chicago because the city possessed a port that could ship the goods further yet. The harbor grew up around the mouth of the Chicago River. "In this narrow, muddy river lies the heart and strength of Chicago," commented a traveller in the mid-1850s. "Dry this up, and Chicago would dry up with it. . . ." Chicagoans wanted no such thing. Harbor improvements dated to the time of Fort Dearborn, when soldiers cut a channel through a sandbar at the mouth of the Chicago River. Water currents there made sandbars a persistent problem; in 1817, one measured some seventy yards in length. Larger ships had to load and unload while anchored a half-mile out in the lake. The process was both inefficient and, given the possibility of lake storms, dangerous.

The federal government funded the first major harbor project in 1833, under the supervision of engineer (and future Confederate president) Jefferson Davis. Still, access to the Chicago River continued to be difficult. To draw attention to the situation, Chicagoans held the city's first great convention in July 1847. The twenty thousand people who attended did not come to select a presidential candidate. Instead, they used the Chicago River and Harbor Convention to demand government support of navigation projects.

The sand ultimately gave way, and Chicago soon became a major port. In 1856, the city shipped its first cargo of wheat direct to Liverpool; six years later, Norway shipped two hundred barrels of herring to Chicago. The city was on its way to becoming an international port, and a busy one. By 1869, three million tons of cargo a year entered the city by water. That translated into a business day which saw as many as three hundred vessels arriving in a twelve-hour period. Then as now, bridges over

the river seemed perpetually confused about whether to stay up or down.

This early Chicago was at times a challenging place to live in or even visit. "In the prairie it rains and thaws incessantly," wrote Ralph Waldo Emerson of his trip in the winter of 1853, "and, if we step off the short street, we go up to the shoulders, perhaps, in mud. . . ." Flat land

with a high water table all too often made an adventure out of a simple walk.

The city found a solution to part of this challenge in the 1850s when it raised the street grade. This action created a new problem, since downtown buildings faced the prospect of raised streets turning valuable first-floor space into basements. Luckily, a newcomer from New

3

York made a name for himself locally by jacking up buildings, as he had along the Erie Canal. In one instance George M. Pullman employed twelve hundred workers and five thousand jackscrews to lift the Tremont House hotel. Pullman would soon become better known through his Pullman Palace Car Company, which helped put overnight train travelers down to sleep.

First, though, someone had to bring a railroad to Chicago. William B. Ogden obliged in 1848. Ogden had arrived from New York thirteen years earlier to assist a brother-in-law who had bought a parcel of land sight-unseen. Finding the property ankle-deep in water, Ogden wrote back, "You have been guilty of the grossest folly." He changed his mind when just one-third of the property sold for $100,000, the original purchase price of the entire property. Ogden decided to stay and take some chances.

Along the way he became Chicago's first mayor and a keen investor; among those benefitting was Cyrus McCormick, inventor of the grain reaper. McCormick realized he could not make money selling the machines from his home in Virginia—there was little market in the South, where cotton was king, and no easy way to ship the reapers to interested buyers in the West. So McCormick decided to relocate to Chicago in 1847. Ogden made the decision along with a loan of $25,000. Business was so good that McCormick repaid the loan plus 100 percent interest two years later. Another of Ogden's shrewd investments helped establish the city's first railroad, the Galena and Chicago Union, in 1848.

The rail line was supposed to connect Chicago with a potential rival on the Mississippi River; at the time, Galena was the center of a prosperous lead-mining region. When it opened in the autumn of 1848, the Galena and Chicago Union had all of ten miles of track leading west out of Chicago to the Des Plaines River. The inaugural run brought back a load of wheat, and that was enough. "Chicago had become Chicago," as journalists Lloyd Lewis and Henry Justin Smith noted.

Already by 1847, at least one member of the Chicago Harbor and River Convention foresaw what water and rail transportation would mean to the city. Judge Jesse B. Thomas predicted they "will at once, and by magic, change the conditions and prospects of our city; increase its population; introduce capital . . . ; enlarge every avenue of commerce; and promote the growth of manufactures." The railroad especially connected Chicago to an emerging national economy. People travelling overland from New York to Chicago in 1830 could not expect to reach their destination in under three weeks; by 1857, the railroad reduced the same trip to just two days.

Suddenly, the railroad became cutting-edge technology, and, by virtue of central location, Chicago was its home. Where only the Galena and Chicago Union entered the city in 1850, ten major lines had arrived by 1856. Some six

Within forty years of their introduction in Chicago, steam engines were an everyday—though impressive—part of city life. These Illinois Central Locomotives at Randolph Street indicate as much.

This bird's-eye view in 1871 offers a booster's portrait of Chicago—sprawling, busy and prosperous. The water was not nearly as clean as the illustration suggests.

The Great Chicago Fire devastated the downtown area around Wabash Avenue, but the fire could not alter the reasons the city became a transportation and manufacturing center. The quick rebuilding and continued expansion only added to Chicago's reputation.

thousand miles of track would cross metropolitan Chicago by the early twentieth century, with 1,300 passenger trains alone moving through the city.

Water and rail transportation made Chicago bloom. A place of 30 residents in 1829 grew to 30,000 in 1850 and just under 300,000 twenty years later. Even the Great Fire of 1871 could only delay, not end, such growth. The fire destroyed 1,688 acres valued at $200 million, at the rate of $125,000 a minute according to the Board of Public Works. Yet the catastrophe did not stop John Stephen Wright from boost-

ing his city: "Chicago will have more men, more money, more business, within five years than she would have had without the fire." The next census would verify the accuracy of Wright's prediction. By decade's end, the city's population exceeded a half-million people.

In Chicago one business activity fed another. The lumber yards located along the south branch of the river were but one example. "The harbor is choked with arriving timber vessels," the historian James Parton wrote in 1867, "[and] timber trains snort over the prairie in every direction." Related firms moved nearby for access to materials. Mills, furniture makers, wagon and ship builders, even a company offering prefabricated housing, all owed their existence to the port of Chicago.

The railroad had an even more profound effect as Chicago began to process the items delivered. Christmas Day 1865 marked the beginning of the greatest such activity when the Union Stock Yards opened. Packers like Armour, Morris and Swift would become household names for consumer and worker alike. Americans were so fascinated by this new enterprise that over one million people who attended the 1893 World's Fair also visited Chicago's stockyards.

Historian Robert Slayton describes the industry: "By 1910 the complex of yards, industries, banks and other structures—known collectively as 'the Yards'—covered 500 acres, had 13,000 pens, 300 miles of railroad tracks, 25 miles of streets, 50 miles of sewers, 90 miles of pipes and 10,000 hydrants." Nine years later, nearly fifteen million animals were rendered into meat and some forty by-products. The packers indeed "used every part of the hog but the squeal" and in so doing provided work for over forty-five thousand people in 1919.

Railroads connected the Great Plains to this faraway metropolis. Farmers and ranchers struggled to raise their crops and livestock for the Chicago market amidst conditions in which at times it seemed "the [grass]hoppers left

"The harbor is choked with arriving timber vessels; timber trains snort over the prairie in every direction," wrote historian James Parton in 1867. Wood was only one of the products Chicago sold to the people of the Great Plains.

Already by the 1880s the Chicago Stock Yards were providing meat to Americans nationwide. The Yards proved a popular destination for visitors to the 1893 World's Fair.

behind nothing but the mortgage." But no dugout or sod house suffered total isolation so long as the family had a mail-order catalogue.

An order form all but put them in downtown Chicago while Montgomery Ward and Sears, Roebuck made a shopping trip virtually unnecessary. Chicago catalogue houses became both supplier and friend. "I suppose you wonder why we haven't ordered anything from you since the fall," wrote a farmer to Montgomery Ward. Times had been hard, "and there was the doctor bill. But now, thank God, that is paid and we are all well again, and we have a fine new baby boy, and please send plush bonnet number 29d8077." And who but a friend would promise satisfaction or your money back, as Sears did?

Sears satisfied customers through its massive catalogue center on the West Side: seven thousand men worked around the clock for a year to erect Arthington Sears. The facility would have been incomplete, of course, without rail service. Access to more than thirty rail lines made the company that much closer to customers who dreamed of catalogue wonders.

The railroad made warehouses and grain elevators staples of the Chicago skyline; it also mandated the building of some of the city's finest architecture. Hamlin Garland, who became known for realistic stories and novels about frontier life, arrived in Chicago by train. Garland had never visited a great city and wondered what he would find. "Soon the straggling farm-houses thickened into groups, the villages merged into suburban towns, and the train began to clatter through" freight yards. Finally, "it plunged into a huge, dark and noisy shed and came to a halt. . . ." For countless travellers, the trip ended at a train station of breathtaking grandeur.

It might have been the Dearborn Street station with its distinctive clock tower or the Grand Central, where an 11,000 pound bell rang out the time. The North Western Station was designed to welcome as many as 250,000 visitors daily, while Union Station showered sunlight into its waiting room from a skylight 112 feet overhead. The Illinois Central Station on Twelfth Street offered something else—a taste of freedom.

The Illinois Central, which ran due south to New Orleans, became a highway in the first part of the twentieth century for African Americans seeking a better life. "You could not rest in your bed at night for Chicago," said one Mississippian. The price of a ticket allowed a person to shout from the train, "Goodbye, bo, I'm bound for the promised land."

One man made the trip north from New Orleans in 1922. A friend was supposed to meet

The Illinois Central railroad station at Twelfth Street and Michigan, designed by Bradford L. Gilbert in 1892. The station welcomed Louis Armstrong and other African Americans who left the South for the opportunity promised by Chicago and other Northern cities in the first half of the twentieth century.

him at the Illinois Central station but had not yet arrived. The newcomer grew worried. "I [had] never seen a city that big," he recalled. "All those tall buildings. I thought they were universities. I said, no, this is the wrong city. I was fixing to take the next train back home. . . ." But just as William Ogden had nearly a century before, trumpeter Louis Armstrong decided to stay.

Chicago commerce manifested itself in other buildings, like its hotels and department stores. The opulent grand dining room of the Palmer House—with gilded Corinthian columns and marble floor—was the setting of a banquet honoring former president Ulysses S. Grant in 1879; the ballroom of the Sherman House served a similar role for Buffalo Bill Cody thirty-five years later. Lesser known visitors could enjoy the same luxurious accommodations or stay at hotels like the Auditorium or the LaSalle.

And they could shop in splendor. Architect Louis Sullivan framed the exterior first two floors of the Schlesinger and Mayer Store (later Carson Pirie Scott) at State and Madison with a lush, ornamental grillwork. The display window thus was transformed into a work of art, the elements of which could be bought inside. Up the street from Carson's stood Marshall Field and Company, in the words of one critic, "an exposition, a school of courtesy, a museum of modern commerce" with floor space totalling close to forty acres. The trading post had indeed grown up.

Sara Jane Lippincott discovered this during her visit from England in 1870. "The growth of this city is one of the most amazing things in the history of modern civilization," she thought. To Lippincott, the vibrancy of Chicago made it "the lightning city." The image held into the next century. "Nowhere else is there such human voltage," Newton Dent wrote in 1907. It was as if the place had a pulse to it. Water and rail transportation, commerce and the industry that followed all combined to endow Chicago with a unique energy.

But not all observers were impressed with what they saw. Rudyard Kipling visited, only to be staggered by the experience: "Having seen it, I urgently desire never to see it again. It is inhabited by savages." Visitor Giuseppe Giacosa found the people less offensive than the air they breathed. "During my stay of one week," he wrote, "I did not see in Chicago anything but darkness: smoke, clouds, dirt and an extraordinary number of sad and grieved persons."

Chicagoans were long accustomed to such criticisms. A city did not rise out of the mud (and later, the ashes) almost overnight without incurring the envy of neighbors. However, there was a growing sense that the city did need fixing. Dr. Frank Felter estimated in 1900 that if the entire city had the density of an average slum neighborhood, the city would have a population of thirty-two million. If it had overall the density of the city's most crowded areas, Felter estimated further, the population would equal that of the entire Western Hemisphere.

The rush to develop carried other consequences, including the air pollution that Giuseppe Giacosa noted with such displeasure. The

The grand parlor of the Palmer House in 1878 may have resembled a European palace, but Chicago defined nobility more in terms of individual talent than birth. The city offered ways to make money; a downtown hotel was one of the places to spend it.

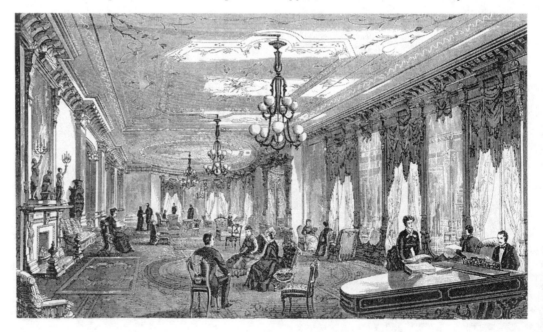

water was even worse. Sewers that emptied into the Chicago River then flowed into and polluted Lake Michigan. The more the city grew, the worse water pollution became, and the harder it was to insure a safe drinking supply. The city responded in 1871 by reversing the flow of the river away from the lake through an enlarged Illinois and Michigan Canal. Sewage was to become the problem of people living downstream.

Industry and nature conspired against any such solution. The meatpackers in particular continued to discharge wastes into a section of the south branch of the river. "The river stinks," the *Chicago Times* complained. "The air stinks. People's clothing, permeated by the foul atmosphere, stinks. . . ." With factories also polluting the river's north branch, the flow reversal had little chance of succeeding.

Bad weather twice overwhelmed the system. Heavy rains in 1879 caused the river to flow into the lake for thirty straight days. Six years later, in August 1885, a downpour of five and a half inches again backed up the river; the

The building of the Sanitary and Ship Canal was an engineering feat to rival that of the Panama Canal. The project was the first major attempt to protect Chicago's drinking supply. The canal also left Chicagoans hopeful they could address the problems resulting from unplanned growth.

Michigan Avenue looking north to Randolph Street, 1858. Chicago paid a price for economic development in the nineteenth century. When the city granted the Illinois Central access to downtown via the lakefront in 1852, people soon realized that trains were more than a passive intrusion. The lesson served as an impetus for treating the lakeshore as a public asset to be protected.

sewage discharge reached the city's only water intake crib. An estimated twelve percent of the people in the city died from diseases carried in the contaminated water. These acts of nature were warning enough, and the Sanitary District of Chicago (now the Metropolitan Water Reclamation District of Greater Chicago) was created in 1889 to insure a safe water supply.

The district began work on the Sanitary and Ship Canal in 1892. The twenty-eight-mile canal was wider than the Suez Canal and forced the excavation of more earth and rock than the Panama Canal required. As in 1871, the canal reversed the flow of the Chicago River away from Lake Michigan; the increased water flow helped break down sewage flowing through the canal. However, water pollution continued to trouble Chicago. As late as 1929, packing houses were pouring over 131,000 pounds of matter a day into city sewers. The fight for a clean environment would be a lengthy one.

Chicago had learned as much with the lakefront. In the rush to develop transportation, the city in 1852 granted a right-of-way to the Illinois Central to run its tracks along the shore from Twenty-second Street to Randolph; in return, the railroad promised to build a breakwater to protect the area. An act passed by the General Assembly in 1867 further gave the railroad use of "a portion of the submerged lands and lake park grounds lying on and adjacent to the shore of Lake Michigan" for development. The assembly overturned the measure five years later, the railroad sued, and the issue was not resolved until 1910, when the Supreme Court ruled the legislature had the power to reverse itself.

In cities like Boston and New York, the waterfront had been given over to development with little question. Chicago was to be different.

As early as the 1830s, civic leaders made sure that some of the property from Fort Dearborn became public land, along with the lakefront east of Michigan Avenue from Twelfth Street to Madison. When a park system was established for the South Side in 1869, Frederick Law Olmsted and Calvert Vaux, creators of New York's Central Park, were hired for the design work. For a city that valued its public space, something about coal cinders from a railroad on the lake shore did not seem quite right.

Journalist Finley Peter Dunne caught the mood in a newspaper column from 1895. Dunne was famous for his creation of Mr. Dooley, a Bridgeport saloonkeeper who dispensed wisdom and drinks in equal measure. Mr. Dooley related the comments of a patron that the Illinois Central had written a new catechism. It taught Chicagoans to recite that they were made by the railroad for the purpose "That I might know it, love it, an' serve it all me days." Readers may have thought otherwise.

As they entered the twentieth century, Chicagoans wanted a city safe, pleasant and prosperous. Their leaders had more ambitious plans: Chicago would not merely be a leading metropolis of the Midwest or even the United States but of the world, with water—again—playing a key role. "The manifest destiny of Chicago is that she shall become the commercial focus between the rich central plain and all the rest of the world," wrote J. Paul Goode in 1909. "To do this, one absolutely essential step is plain—Chicago must become her own seaport."

Ultimately, this desire for greater commerce fused with the drive for a better urban environment. The result was a grand municipal pier not far from the home of Jean Baptiste Point du Sable.

Planning Several Piers, Building One

2

Navy Pier evolved from the work of two separate—and at times antagonistic—planning groups. In January 1908 Mayor Fred Busse appointed a Harbor Commission to consider expanding Chicago's port facilities. Busse informed the city council, "It is a notorious fact that the lake commerce of Chicago, once the pride and boast of this city, has been steadily decreasing for a number of years." At the same time, the Chicago Commercial Club was readying a report that would forever change the way the city looked at itself.

Chicago architect Daniel Burnham, the creative force behind that work, had long been interested in city planning. Burnham and the Merchants' Club agreed in 1906 to present a plan for managing growth in the Chicago region. The group soon merged with the Commercial Club, which took on the task of publishing the report in 1909.

Burnham did not intend just to offer a few modest suggestions. He proposed a massive reordering of the city and outlying region. This vision was the logical extension of Burnham's personal philosophy. "Make no little plans," Burnham counselled, "they have no magic to stir men's blood and probably themselves will not be realized. Make big plans; aim high in hope and work remembering that a noble, logical diagram once recorded will never die, but long after we are gone will be a living thing. . . ." The architect could do no less for a city he believed would attain a population in excess of thirteen million people by 1952.

Burnham was an eighth-generation American who came with his family to Chicago from New York in the 1850s. As a young man, Burnham was undecided on a career. That uncertainty in 1869 led him to Nevada, where he tried his hand at silver prospecting and politics. The failure to find another Comstock Lode or win election to the state senate brought Burnham back to Chicago. Architecture had been one of the few areas of study that interested him as a student. So Burnham decided to learn the profession while working for several Chicago architects. In 1873 the twenty-seven-year-

old felt confident enough to enter into practice with partner John Wellborn Root.

For the next eighteen years, Burnham and Root would gain fame for such designs as the Rookery and Monadnock buildings downtown and St. Gabriel's Church on the South Side. "Yours is a good concern to do business with," one client wrote the firm. "You not only can make a good picture of a house, but you can build a good one. . . ." That ability to satisfy contributed to Burnham and Root's selection as consulting architects for the World's Columbian Exposition or World's Fair, to celebrate the four hundredth anniversary of the voyage by Christopher Columbus to the New World; Burnham was named chief of construction in 1890. The fair proved a defining moment both for the city and Daniel Burnham.

Chicagoans wanted to host the fair to show that they had fully recovered from the Great Fire and, more important, to prove the city had more to offer visitors than just stockyards or railroads. Nationwide, there were doubters like editor Charles A. Dana, who told readers of the *New York Sun* to ignore "the nonsensical claims of that windy city. Its people could not build a World's Fair even if they won it." Dana proved mistaken. Chicago won the ensuing national competition for site selection, along with its Windy City nickname.

John Root's sudden death in 1891 left Burnham in charge of the construction of some two hundred buildings on the 633-acre site in Jackson Park. Burnham rose to the occasion as he coordinated the design and construction of what became known as the White City, for the white paint used on the buildings. About twentyseven million people visited the fairgrounds from May to October 1893. The young Hamlin Garland was among them. The fair so overwhelmed Garland that he wrote his father on the Great Plains, "Sell the cook stove if necessary and come. You **must** see this fair." Many of those who did were overwhelmed by the fair's size. It was estimated that a person who wanted to see everything quickly would have to spend about three weeks at the fair and walk more than 150 miles.

Chicago architect Daniel Burnham (1846–1912), who believed that a big plan done well "will never die, but long after we are gone will be a living thing, asserting itself with evergrowing insistency." Burnham's Plan of Chicago placed a municipal pier at Chicago Avenue, with another at Twenty–second Street.

While most visitors were struck by the fair's neoclassical architecture, the Columbian Exposition embodied as much the spirit of Thomas Edison as ancient Rome. Electricity and invention were everywhere. Fairgoers noted the "wondrous enchantment of the night illumination" of the fairgrounds; a passenger pier on Lake Michigan included an electrically powered movable sidewalk; and electric lights outlined one of the fair's greatest attractions, the rotating wheel of George W. G. Ferris, which rose 250 feet into the air. Hezekiah Butterworth described the thrill of a ride on the Ferris Wheel: "The horizon grew; the great blue lake, the White City in dazzling whiteness, moved into view, and then sank downward. . . ."

Burnham was much like the fair he helped build, conservative on the surface, innovative underneath. Architect Louis Sullivan condemned the fair for popularizing long-outdated building styles, what Sullivan dismissed as "the bogus antique." Burnham took away different lessons. Where Sullivan championed the right of the individual architect working alone, Burnham was intrigued by the way a unified style of architecture offered a sense of design cohesion. He also discovered that a well-planned site could accommodate great numbers, with the fair attracting a one-day record in excess of 700,000 visitors. The experience encouraged Burnham to use a similar approach to conceptualizing an entire city, even one filled with smokestacks and cattle.

Following the fair, Burnham no longer devoted himself solely to work on individual buildings. He became a pioneer in the field of urban planning, with proposals for Washington, D.C.; Cleveland; San Francisco; and Manila and Baguio in the Philippines before he began further work on Chicago in 1906. Assisted by Edward H. Bennett, Burnham outlined a series of proposals made necessary because "the time has come to bring order out of the chaos incident to rapid growth, and especially to the influx of people of many nationalities without common traditions or habits of life." The purpose of his plan, Burnham argued, was to create "a well-ordered, convenient and unified city."

Burnham focussed much of his attention on transportation: "The plan frankly takes into consideration the fact that the American city, and Chicago preeminently, is a center of industry and traffic." The problem was traffic flow, or rather its lack. To remedy that, Burnham proposed a regional highway system; a massive reordering of the city's streets, including diagonal routes and Congress Street as a "broad cross avenue" to form the city's "backbone"; and a consolidation of freight and passenger rail traffic. Burnham reminded businessmen reluctant to make these changes "that what is for the greatest advantage to the city as a whole will also be of the greatest benefit to the transportation lines both collectively and individually."

The Chicago Plan would have been judged important simply as a transportation study, yet

The Basin and the Court of Honor at the World's Columbian Exposition; the statue of the Republic is in the foreground opposite the Administration Building. His experience as the fair's chief of construction led Daniel Burnham to urban planning.

Burnham intended far more. He wrote, "To love and render service to one's city, to have a part in its advancement, to seek to better its conditions and to promote its highest interests—these are both the duty and the privilege of the patriot . . . [during] peace." As such, he could not limit himself to a plan devoted merely to reducing traffic congestion.

Burnham sensed there existed a unique opportunity to reorder the city. Europe was showing the way, especially Paris, whose people "have always supported those who aimed to make their city grand and beautiful." Like his contemporaries, Burnham believed Chicago could rival Berlin, London or Vienna. But he defined success differently: Chicago had to be both a place where people made a good living and where they enjoyed life fully.

Burnham's notion of the good life was shaped by an almost-mystical view of nature and its restorative powers. "Natural scenery furnishes the contrasting element to the artificiality of the city," Burnham wrote. Towards that end, he proposed to blanket his city with park land, starting at the shore line. Where others saw a resource for potential commercial development, Burnham declared, "The lake front by right belongs to the people."

Burnham hoped to develop the lakefront for the public good with a new outer shore that would create a series of lagoons; in addition, a string of islands would stretch from about Fifty-ninth Street north to Wilmette. Such a project was "dictated by considerations of health and enjoyment." Burnham fully intended to recreate an experience more commonly found on the Thames, the Seine or the canals of Venice: "When this parkway shall be created, our people will stay here, and others will come to dwell among us—the people who now spend time and large amounts of money in Paris, in Vienna and on the Riviera."

The lakeshore east of downtown received special attention. There were to be two great "public recreation piers," one at Chicago Avenue, the other at Twenty-second Street; they were to reach out a mile and a half into the lake. Further, a recreational harbor was planned for the area between Randolph and Thirteenth Street, with yacht clubs, passenger steamboat landings and lighthouses. This was the backdrop for Grant Park, in turn to be developed as the city's cultural center.

Burnham hoped the plan, which also included a regional forest preserve system and a massive civic center at Congress and Halsted, would convince Chicagoans to embrace his view of the future. "If, therefore, the plan is a good one," he wrote in conclusion, business would thrive "while we and our children can enjoy and improve life as we cannot do now. Then our own people will become home-keepers, and the stranger will seek our gates."

The plan did not stop there. Mayor Fred Busse soon appointed a Chicago Plan Commission, which spread the planning gospel through a movie, slide shows and the public schools. Eighth graders read an adaptation of the Chicago Plan as their civics text. "The children became voters," Lloyd Lewis and Henry Justin

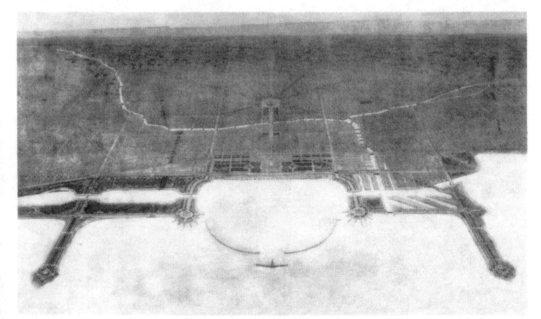

The vision of Daniel Burnham: The city as it would have looked according to the Chicago Plan. The two municipal piers were to be one and a half miles long. Plate 87 from plan of Chicago, 1909. Art Institute of Chicago, Gift of Patrick Shaw 1991.

Smith noted. "When in later years they were presented with ballots including Chicago Plan projects, they voted 'Yes' almost automatically."

Burnham hoped that his plan ultimately would create a sense of civic virtue, particularly among new residents who would pledge themselves to a city so prosperous and beautiful. The Harbor Commission took a more pragmatic approach to its work. Mayor Busse formed the commission to help revive Chicago as a harbor facility. The Chicago Plan, noting that 95 percent "of the entire freight traffic" into or out of the city was by rail, had minimized the role of water transportation in the city's future.

The Harbor Commission disliked the idea of keeping the lakefront free of commercial development. Instead, the commission believed "no park development should be favored which will forever prevent the possibility of utilizing a portion of this area later for harbor purposes." Daniel Burnham did have at least one influence, though. The commission planned big.

"Chicago's manifest destiny is plain," J. Paul Goode wrote in a special report to the commission. The city would exploit a vast inland waterway together with "fleets of ocean-going steamers" that would allow Chicago to challenge the likes of New York, London, Antwerp and Hamburg. "Our future is as great as we are wise enough to make it," Goode advised. "Our limitations are human and social, not in the opportunities nature has given us."

One proposal submitted to the commission reflected in particular this desire to make Chicago a port of the world. Alfred Beirly argued for the construction of a canal, six hundred to seven hundred feet wide, west from the junction of the two branches of the Chicago River. The waterway was to continue west some two and a third miles to Rockwell Street before turning south to the Sanitary and Ship Canal at about Thirty-first Street.

Commissioners no doubt agreed with Beirly's sentiment, "Chicago stands at the very forefront in greatness." They simply were unwilling to undertake such a vast project. Instead, the commission recommended a number of improvements for the Chicago and Calumet Rivers. Also, the lakefront from Randolph Street to Chicago Avenue would be held "for future harbor development" while the shoreline south of Grant Park down to Jackson Park would be subject to joint commercial-public use if necessary.

That recommendation brought a response from the Commercial Club. Rather than develop so much of the shoreline for shipping, the club urged combined use of the municipal pier Daniel Burnham proposed for east of Chicago Avenue. The mile-and-a-half-long pier could include a number of lateral piers on its southerly side. The club believed that such a design would create ten miles of dock frontage for commercial shipping and mean "no further harbor development" would be needed for the shoreline between the Chicago and Calumet Rivers. Despite a plea to remember "the great

Lakefront landfill, 1908. The Chicago Plan envisioned Grant Park as a cultural and recreational center. Daniel Burnham did not want the city's shoreline given over to massive commercial development.

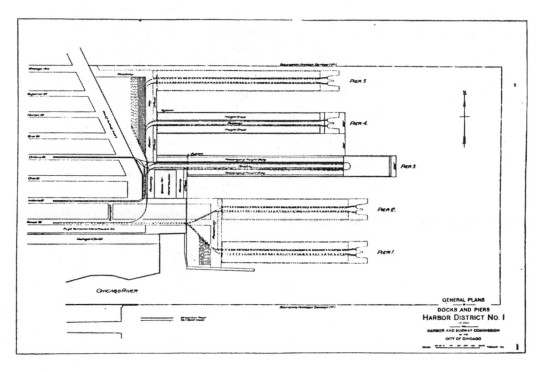

Charles Sumner Frost (1856–1931) designed a pier both to function as a multi-use facility and to symbolize the foresight of city government.

importance of harmonizing the views" of those involved in lakefront planning, the commission rejected the club's alternative.

Most Chicagoans probably saw no contradiction in supporting both the Harbor Commission and the Chicago Plan. Each called for harbor development. The commission offered a comprehensive approach, focussed and full of promise. The Chicago Plan, for all of its scope, was not an ironclad document requiring absolute compliance. "It is not to be expected that any plan devised while as yet few civic problems have received final solution will be perfect in all its details," Daniel Burnham himself admitted in the introduction. So the initial advantage lay with the Harbor Commission, with one important consolation for proponents of the Chicago Plan. Construction would proceed only one pier at a time. Conditions might change before the building of another.

The General Assembly approved enabling legislation for harbor development in the summer of 1911. Next, the city council created a Harbor and Subway Commission to coordinate the work. (The commission also was to deal with the near-impossible problem of subway construction, which would not begin until 1938.) As originally conceived by the council, the new commission would be responsible for five harbor districts. Municipal Pier was to be one of five structures in Harbor District No. 1.

In 1913 the commission chose architect Charles Sumner Frost to design the pier. Like William Ogden, Daniel Burnham and other Chicagoans born in the nineteenth century, Frost came from the East. He was born in Lewiston, Maine, in 1856. After graduating from Massachusetts Institute of Technology, he worked in the Boston architectural firm of Peabody and Stearns. Frost arrived in Chicago in 1882 and went into partnership with Henry Ives Cobb. Frost and Cobb are perhaps best known for the castle-like Potter Palmer mansion, located on Lake Shore Drive just north of Division Street.

Frost then worked independently from 1889 until 1898, when he and Alfred H. Granger became partners. Granger gave the firm an important perspective derived from his training at the ecole des Beaux-Arts in Paris. With architecture only recently considered a true profession, many American students of the late nineteenth and early twentieth centuries (including, ironically, Louis Sullivan) continued their studies in Paris, where the ecole operated under the direction of the French government.

The ecole's design philosophy was a product of its history, dating to the reign of Louis XIV. "Your Majesty knows that, except for outstanding military engagements, nothing marks the grandeur and spirit of princes more than buildings," wrote Minister of Finance Jean-Baptiste Colbert to the Sun King, "and all posterity measures these qualities by the merit of the splendid houses that they have raised during their lives." The architect was trained to handle large projects in a way that conveyed the power, dignity and wisdom of the state.

Arguably, the greatest Beaux-Arts undertaking took place in Paris from 1854 to 1869. Appointed by emperor Napoleon III, Baron Georges-Eugene Haussmann attempted to modernize what was essentially a medieval city. While not a student of the ecole, Haussmann initiated a series of projects that would give Paris its Beaux-Arts appearance. He constructed a system of boulevards as well as public buildings and monuments; Haussmann also built a water and sanitation system. Paris emerged as a city where residents (not to mention the emperor's troops) could travel easily and live in the most pleasant of surroundings.

The Beaux-Arts exerted considerable influence on Chicago. The Columbian Exposition reflected it in the fair's neoclassical style and the ordering of buildings around a court of honor. As in Paris, the masses of people were impressed. The Beaux-Arts bore just as heavily on the Chicago Plan, which at times verged on a paean to all things Parisian. "The task which Haussmann accomplished for Paris," wrote Daniel Burnham, "corresponds with the work which must be done for Chicago. . . ."

The railroads lent themselves almost naturally to the Beaux-Arts style. By necessity, train stations were large structures whose success depended on their ability to move great numbers of passengers quickly and easily; the Beaux-Arts architect possessed the skills to meet that design requirement. The style also made a good emotional fit for railroad magnates. "Everything that is not nailed down is mine," believed Collis P. Huntington, "and anything I can pry loose is not nailed down." It was only fitting for such robber barons that their railroad stations resemble palaces.

Frost and Granger had designed stations in Omaha, St. Paul and Montreal along with two in Chicago, the LaSalle Street and the Chicago and North Western Stations, the latter of particular interest. The North Western Terminal and its related structures took up thirteen of the complex's forty-three acres. The station was done in the Renaissance style, with an impressive main entrance on Madison Street—a portico including six massive granite columns measuring sixty-one feet in height. And in true Beaux-Arts fashion, the station was functional as well as majestic. The design was geared to accommodate five hundred trains and a quarter-of-a-million passengers daily.

Frost brought the same sensibilities to his work on the pier, which now combined elements of the Chicago Plan with the interests of the Harbor and Subway Commission. The pier was to reflect an enlightened city government through its multi-faceted role as a freight/passenger/recreation facility. Frost accomplished this in ways both subtle and obvious. Any structure that extended 3,000 feet into the lake and was 292 feet wide could not help but appear monumental. Frost

The Chicago and North Western Station, designed by Charles Frost and Alfred Granger. Done in the Beaux–Arts style, the station featured an entrance portico with six granite columns sixty-one feet high.

furthered that feeling with a neoclassical style for the buildings at the head and the east end of the pier. The idea was to impress visitors with what they saw both up close and at a distance.

The design also included terra cotta ornamentation rich in symbolism. Such figures as a frog, sea horse, turtle, lily and cattails conveyed the sense that the pier was part of the lakeshore. A Native American and sheaf of wheat connected the pier to Chicago's past. Use of the city seal also left no doubt that this was a project that the people of Chicago should take pride in.

The pier was built at the foot of Grand Ave-nue. The western-most building was the head house, or general offices. Like all the pier facilities excepting the freight and passenger buildings, the head house was a steel-frame structure clad in red brick. The offices were flanked by two towers, each holding a gravity tank with a sixty-thousand-gallon capacity to feed the pier's fire-sprinkler system.

Next came the freight and passenger buildings. Actually, these were two wings on either side of the pier, each 2,340 feet by 100 feet. The wings, or sheds, were separated by an interior roadway 80 feet wide; railroad tracks were added to this area later. The first floor of the

Substructure work on the pier in May 1914 attracted at least one well-dressed onlooker (*lower left*). The pier's foundation and substructure had to withstand a Lake Michigan that was not always this placid. *Photo courtesy of Great Lakes Dredge and Dock Company.*

Timber foundation piles used for supporting pier buildings. Over twenty thousand pilings were used. *Photo courtesy of Great Lakes Dredge and Dock Company.*

largely glass and steel structure was devoted to freight, the second to passengers who either walked in through the head house or rode to a particular boat on the Grand Avenue streetcar; the trolley continued onto the pier around an elevated interior loop. Passengers were able to board their steamers directly from the second floor of the building. There was also a boardwalk on the roof of each shed for pedestrians to reach the pier's east end.

Diver preparing to work on pier substructure, June 1914. Construction techniques had advanced since the building of the Illinois and Michigan Canal, but it was still dangerous work. *Photo courtesy of Great Lakes Dredge and Dock Company.*

The twin sheds of the freight and passenger buildings under construction. Two trains forty cars long were needed to haul just the sash and doors used on the pier's various structures.

Construction of the pier, especially the freight and passenger buildings, required special materials. They arrived on two trains, each forty cars long, to carry the necessary sash and doors. The pier used 150,000 square feet of sash along with 200 swinging and 2,808 sliding doors, the tracks for which would have extended ten miles if laid in a straight line. Eighteen miles of door trimmings and 625 tons of kick plates for lower door protection also

The weather did not always cooperate during the pier's construction. This scene is New Year's Eve, 1914. *Courtesy of* The Municipal Library, Chicago City Hall.

Head house under construction, February 1915. Each of the towers would hold a sixty-thousand-gallon tank for a sprinkler system to protect the complex.

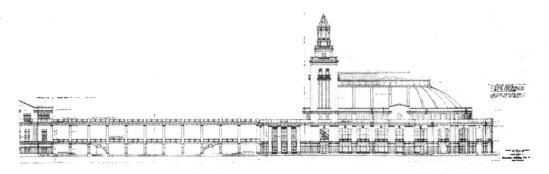

were used. The Detroit Steel Products Company was certain it had filled "the largest single order for steel sash ever placed with any manufacturer." An additional fifteen rail cars were needed to carry the glass and another two for the putty. In all, the pier was outfitted with over eighty thousand window panes.

Directly to the east of the sheds was the terminal building, about 245 feet by 30 feet. Located here were information offices, restrooms, first-aid station, restaurant and roof garden. An open air shelter building, 80 feet by 220 feet and two stories high plus a roof deck, connected the terminal building to the concert hall.

The hall, at the eastern end of the pier, was a half-shell measuring 150 feet by 138 feet, with a domed ceiling 100 feet high. Frost rendered the concert hall, with room for 4,000 people, into an exceptional space. He used radial steel trusses shaped as half-arches to carry the dome and above that located a skylight supported by trusses. The hall included two 165-foot-tall observation towers.

"The dance and music pavilion, the dining halls, shelter building, loggias and terraces are conceived with a sense of spacious beauty hard to rival," a city pamphlet declared. "The flag staffs topped with golden eagles, the wrought iron lamp posts, the rostral columns and balustrades of the furthermost terrace are reminiscent of Venice and the Trocadero at Paris." This was no idle boast. The outline of the concert hall and observation towers together with seating capacity resembled that of the theatre portion of the Trocadero Palace, built for the Exposition of 1878. Frost may have found that some imitation of a Paris building was the highest form of flattery.

The question of design influences would have mattered little without the work of Edward C. Shankland, a member of the Harbor and Subway Commission as well as its chief engineer. Shankland had worked on large projects since at least the early 1890s, when he served as chief engineer for the Columbian Exposition; he also had worked with Frost and Granger on the LaSalle Street and North Western stations. Shankland confronted a basic challenge with the pier—how to keep the lake from pounding it into the water.

The solution lay in the substructure and foundation, consisting of over twenty thousand pilings of Oregon timber. This work, begun in April 1914, included installing steel tie-rods to keep the various pilings anchored in place. The concrete foundation rested on piles driven twenty to twenty-seven feet down, with a triple row of piles supporting the concrete dock walls. Pilings also formed a border around the pier to hold a protective fill of clay, rock and sand. The border in turn was buttressed by loose rock; in addition, pilings supported the steel columns of the pier buildings. At its completion, the pier's engineering work was virtually invisible. Without it, the pier would have been a costly failure.

The project's official designation was Municipal Pier No. 2. But there would be no other piers, nor as proposed in 1912, an elevated moving sidewalk from Franklin Street to the pier's eastern end. Money played a part in ending further work. The pier cost $4.5 million to construct. With inflation reaching 100 percent for the period 1913–18, any new structure would have cost about double. And there was the question of need. The twentieth century was proving Daniel Burnham right. Chicago would continue to handle an immense volume of freight, most of which came by rail, not water.

Still, Chicago found itself with an incredible asset, described by one critic who saw it as a microcosm for the city itself: "It is big in idea," wrote Ira Hoover, "and this conception has been transplanted into concrete, brick and steel with a courage of which you can form no conception save by seeing with your own eyes." Curiosity would bring some people out to the pier, but others would need a stronger reason. Eventually, a politician known for his size and controversy would give it to them.

The First Golden Age

3

"Picnic Boat," Carl Sandburg

Sunday night and the park
    policemen tell each other it is
    dark as a stack of black cats
    on Lake Michigan.
A big picnic boat comes home to
    Chicago from the peach farms
    of Saugatuck.
Hundreds of electric bulbs break
    the night's darkness, a flock
    of red and yellow birds with
    wings at a standstill.

Running along the deck-railings
    are festoons and leaping in
    curves are loops of light from
    prow and stern to the tall
    smokestacks.
Over the hoarse crunch of
    waves at my pier comes a
    hoarse answer in the rhyth-
    mic oompa of the brasses play-
    ing a Polish folk-song for the
    home-comers.

Chicago was in no mood to wait for the sched-uled completion of Municipal Pier in mid-July 1916. Instead, fifty thousand people used the Fourth of July as an excuse to visit. The holiday was "an impromptu dedication," reported the *Tribune*, adding that "no city in the world has any structure on a waterfront that compares with the new Municipal Pier, [as] was appar-ently fully appreciated by the joyous thousands who went to take a peep at things and remained all day to enjoy themselves." When the temper-ature reached 101.7 degrees on July 30th, the visitors had incentive to return, both for the pier and the possibility of a cooling lake breeze.

The pier's opening offered a diversion from the anxiety that had been building for two years. The world had gone to war in 1914, and Chicagoans could not easily isolate themselves from it. Some 67 percent of the city's 2.4 million people were made up of immigrants and their children who worried over the fate of family and friends left behind. Even those Chicagoans without any direct connection felt the tension. Ultimately, the United States would declare war on Imperial Germany in April 1917. And so Chicago—including its new Municipal Pier—joined the effort to make the world safe for democracy.

Since the new pier was such an imposing symbol of government, it offered the perfect site for a recruiting center. In addition, military and civilian personnel trained on the grounds.

Army, Navy, Red Cross—all utilized the pier to get ready for war. By one account, the pier "was virtually an armed camp with gun-boats and cruisers growling defiance from the water's side."

The pier had at least two other wartime uses. One of the towers on the east end became a carrier-pigeon station while another area served as a detention camp. In July 1918, the American Protective League (a volunteer auxil-iary of the Justice Department) conducted a massive sweep of the city in search of draft resisters. Agents sealed off Cubs' Park during a doubleheader with the Boston Braves to check on the military status of draft-age men in the stands. Another raid centered on the Barnum and Bailey Circus at the White City Amusement Park on the South Side. In all, some 200,000 men were questioned. Those detained were sent to Municipal Pier.

A jail by the lake did not fit into the pier's long-term future. Both during and after the war, city officials operated the pier as a place for virtuous play and recreation, in keeping with the moral climate of the Progressive Era. The poor, Jane Addams wrote, "live for the moment [in slums] side by side, many of them without knowledge of each other, without fel-lowship, without local tradition or public spirit, without social organization of any kind." Addams was one of many social reformers who advocated establishing places where people

The auditorium at Municipal Pier was often used for civic functions, both during war and peacetime.

could enjoy themselves without fear of violence or moral corruption. The saloon and dance hall did not qualify for obvious reasons, and, for children, the streets were not much better.

Reformers had championed the settlement house, park and playground as alternatives; Municipal Pier now could be another. Following the war, the pier emerged as a kind of continuing education center for adult and child alike. To publicize this role, the city printed a pamphlet: SPEND YOUR VACATION ON THE $5,000,000 **MUNICIPAL PIER**/ Boating Fishing Dancing Music/ One Mile in the Lake/ BUILT BY THE CITY AND OWNED BY THE CITY/**FOR THE PEOPLE**.

No one would confuse Chicago with Atlantic City, not after visiting the art room in the pier's auditorium. The publicity pamphlet explained how paintings on display "tell their story to the plain citizen as well as to the highbrow," as did perhaps the exhibits on natural history from the Field Museum. The auditorium itself featured theatre, music and special presentations. Chicago was the beneficiary of auditorium programs that contributed "to the physical, mental and moral welfare of its citizens."

Youngsters received special attention with a city-subsidized Children's Civic Theatre run by the Chicago Drama League. The hope was that the performing arts would counter the lure of the streets. Rather than become juvenile delinquents, children would learn self-expression, teamwork and other skills along with an appreciation of the arts. Instruction took place afternoons in the summer. The pier auditorium was devoted to children who worked on plays, dancing, pantomime and storytelling. Youngsters staged plays for the public on Wednesdays and put on a Gala for the Drama League in August.

According to the publicity pamphlet, just walking the pier promised substantial benefits. "Roaming and resting on the pier in the midst of a wealth of sunshine and pure air is conducive to health and happiness to such an extent that one soon feels the necessity for something substantial to eat." The cafeteria-restaurant provided it "at prices within the reach of all."

The roof garden was yet another area of the pier with the power to raise a person's spirits. "Here," the pamphlet continued, "in the balmy breezes of summer afternoons and evenings, to the strains of classical, popular and patriotic music, refreshments are served at moderate prices." The space provided a sense of what

SPEND YOUR VACATION ON THE

$5,000,000

MUNICIPAL PIER

BOATING
FISHING

DANCING
MUSIC

ONE MILE IN THE LAKE

BUILT BY THE CITY AND OWNED BY THE CITY FOR THE PEOPLE

Daniel Burnham intended in his plan: "From this point a truly Venetian scene presents itself as the last rays of the sun lose themselves in a gorgeous sunset over the boats and piers in the distance."

This was Municipal Pier, open year round with the summer season extending from Decoration (now Memorial) Day to Labor Day. Seemingly every offering was conducive to civic virtue. The theatre audiences enjoyed themselves while "developing unconsciously [the] community spirit and viewpoint which are the hope of democracy in our big city." Community singing broke down "those stupid barriers that commonly isolate" people. Activities for chil-

Front cover of a tourist pamphlet promoting Municipal Pier. Chicago may have been an industrial city, but civic leaders hoped the pier would prove popular as a vacation destination.

23

There was a strong reform emphasis on organized play at the pier, but children could find other diversions like the carousel.

dren were shaped "to keep them occupied in a wholesome, clean atmosphere, and to give them every opportunity toward healthful play and tutoring." And the dances at the pier took place "with all objectionable features eliminated."

The *Chicago Evening Post* approved of the format. "The joy of entertainment in the drama, music, the dance and the interest in pictures and sculpture awakens pleasant thought, making the tired worker throw off his worries and realize that the struggle for existence is but one phase of living," an editorial noted. "As a stimulus of recreative activities of the higher order, the Municipal Pier is taking the lead these days." But for William Hale "Big Bill" Thompson, moral uplift was not enough. The pier had to benefit him personally as mayor.

Thompson served three terms (1915–1923, 1927–1931) in office before retiring as Chicago's most controversial if not its best mayor. In many ways, Thompson was a blue blood gone bad. Born on prestigious Beacon Street in Boston, he came with his family to Chicago at the age of two in 1869. Like Daniel Burnham, Thompson was drawn to the West, where he stayed part of each year beginning at the age of fourteen. Thompson might have been entirely satisfied spending the rest of his life managing

a family ranch in western Nebraska, but his father's sudden death in 1891 forced a return to Chicago. Thompson adopted one piece of the West, a trademark Stetson, that accompanied him throughout his public life.

Thompson won his first term running as a self-styled reformer. But allegations of corruption followed within months, and they seemed without end for the next sixteen years. The most damning involved Thompson and organized crime. The mayor of Chicago was reputed to be in the pocket of Al Capone.

Thompson gained particular notoriety during the First World War. He had criticized the declaration of war; refused to extend a formal invitation to a visiting Allied delegation that included the French war hero Marshal Joseph Joffre; and allowed an antiwar group to meet in Chicago after other cities had refused it permission. (Quite secretly, Thompson also made sure to cooperate with federal authorities in gathering information on war protestors in the city.) Thompson thought he could win election to the Senate with such appeals to Midwestern isolationism, only to lose the 1918 Republican primary. And, although he won a second term as mayor in 1919, the race riot that summer had tarnished his reputation.

Other politicians might have despaired in

JULY 30th to
AUGUST 14th
1921
CHICAGO

ADMISSION
50¢

The PAGEANT
of PROGRESS
EXPOSITION

This program cover suggested
the Pageant of Progress was a
civic undertaking, while in
fact it was privately organized.

25 SHOWS IN ONE AT THE PAGEANT OF PROGRESS EXPOSITION ON CHICAGO'S $5,000,000 MUNICIPAL PIER
SWEPT BY COOL BREEZES — JULY 30th to AUGUST 14th 1921

GORGEOUS FIREWORKS DISPLAY

AEROPLANES & PIGEON RACE

MUSICAL CONCERTS

U.S. LIFE GUARD'S EXHIBITION

INTERNATIONAL TYPEWRITER CONTESTS

BEAUTIFUL FASHION SHOW

WISCONSIN DAY

FIRE BOAT EXHIBITION

ILLINOIS DAY

DIVING CONTEST

NAVY BALL

CROWNING CHICAGO'S QUEEN

MAMMOTH NAVAL MANEUVERS

CHINESE DAY

SPECTACULAR STREET PARADES

FIFTY THOUSAND PEOPLE DANCING ON MICHIGAN BOULEVARD

DIVING IN A SHEET OF FLAME

ELEVEN MEN PARACHUTING FROM ONE HYDROPLANE

3½ Miles of Industrial Exhibits

1. Paper Products-Advertising-Office
2. Furniture — Rugs — Shoes
3. General Merchandise
4. Horticulture-Educational
5. Food Products 6. Milk-Milk Products
7. Medical Science-Child Hygiene
8. Public Health-Sanitation 9. Furs
10. Government Dept.-Historical-Chemical Toys-Educational
11. School Industries
12. Building Industries
13. Electrical Industries-Public Utilities
14. Laundry Appliances
15. Public Safety
16. Automobile Show

this situation, but Thompson persevered according to his motto: "Throw away your hammer! Get a horn! Be a booster for Chicago!" In 1921 he decided the best way to do that—and revive his popularity—was to hold a Pageant of Progress at Municipal Pier. "We'll sell Chicago to Chicagoans and sell Chicago to the outside world," he promised.

Thompson's formula for the Pageant was to jam the pier with exhibits and, if that failed to impress people, provide the entertainment that would. The Pageant would let people take a look at Cyrus McCormick's first reaper, the world's fastest steam locomotive and a line of paper clothing. Or they could watch airplanes, parachutists and mock naval battles, provided they went to Municipal Pier sometime between July 30 and August 14.

Two weeks before the Pageant's opening, Thompson was so confident of success that he removed the old dedication plaque on the pier. It mentioned Carter Harrison II, during whose administration most of the pier's construction had taken place. Big Bill Thompson was not a politician given to sharing publicity, so the new plaque made it appear Municipal Pier was his handiwork alone.

Thompson always thrived on taking politics to the extreme, as when he organized an expedition to the South Seas in search of tree-climbing fish or when he "debated" two caged rats

Mayor William Hale "Big Bill" Thompson used a beauty contest to help maintain interest in the 1921 Pageant of Progress. Here he stands alongside contestant Evelyn Slader, who was already Queen of the Stockyards District.

at a rally. But he was on solid ground in promoting the Pageant of Progress. Chicagoans had supported such exhibitions for decades, from as early as 1872 when the Inter-state Industrial Exposition was organized to publicize the city's recovery from the Great Fire, producing a fair so popular that it became an annual event. The Columbian Exposition was essentially an even bigger trade fair, displays of state-of-the-art

A poster from the 1921 Pageant of Progress.

27

technology housed in buildings made to look ancient. The Pageant of Progress merely took the displays out of mock temples and put them on Municipal Pier.

The Pageant featured two thousand exhibits housed in the sheds of the freight and passenger buildings. The displays in seventeen general categories ranged from paper products, horticulture and food industries to the automobile industry and the manufacture of public safety devices. Exhibitors such as the refrigerator manufacturer who booked enough orders to keep his factory busy for a year came away satisfied.

So did anyone who was curious as to what a house built of monkey wrenches looked like. The Pageant also offered more mainstream attractions like airplane races, nightly firework displays and parachute jumps; nightly dives by Jack "The Human Torch" Turner—who jumped into the water **after** setting his gasoline-soaked swimsuit on fire—defied easy categorization. Meanwhile, the Chicago Plan Commission used the opportunity to distribute 300,000 booklets publicizing its work.

Thompson made sure his pageant succeeded. Activities commenced with a four-mile-long parade through the heart of the city; some 30 percent of Chicago's population lined the streets to watch. Constant coverage in the papers maintained interest, which in turn fed attendance. Those who went found the Pageant anything but dull. There was something sure to amaze: the five thousand Pigeons of Prosperity; a working model of the new Michigan Avenue bridge; or an invention that promised to shrink distance to practically nothing. The Department of Gas and Electricity had linked the pier to city hall by radio.

And unlike other aspects of city life, the Pageant was not a segregated affair. The pier auditorium was filled for an August 7th commemoration honoring the memory of Frederick Douglass, who escaped slavery at age twenty-one to become one of the leading abolitionists and civil rights leaders of the nineteenth century. During the Columbian Exposition, Douglass delivered a speech on "The Race Problem in America." Sitting in the pier auditorium twenty-eight years later, African Americans could measure the progress made since 1893—and the distance still to travel.

Attendance at the Pageant ranged somewhere between one and two million; the single-day record was set on August 7 with 250,000 people (some of whom witnessed the death of a parachutist who crashed into a tower during his descent). Thompson was pleased enough with the public response that he declared the Pageant would become an annual event.

The second fair featured an International Radio Congress and a visit by heavyweight champion Jack Dempsey along with a unique competition. When Jack Turner complained about not being rehired to perform at the Pageant, Thompson arranged a "dive-off" between Turner and his successor, Harold "Stubby" Kruger. Turner won his job back.

However, the second Pageant proved a disappointment. Attendance declined by half, in part because of bad weather and a transportation strike. Ironically, William Hale Thompson also helped kill his own creation. Immediately after the first Pageant closed, questions surfaced over fair revenues and the use of city workers on the pier; technically, the Pageant was a private enterprise, with Thompson listed as one of its officers. The taint of corruption carried over to the second Pageant, which was marred by a Prohibition raid on the roof garden the night before opening. When Thompson decided not to seek re-election in 1923, his successor let the Pageant die.

But Big Bill Thompson's misfortune was not Municipal Pier's. The pier continued as before, although a second Prohibition raid suggested the environment was no longer quite as virtuous. Pier attendance remained steady in the years following the Pageants and reached 3.2 million in 1926. Children had their own reasons for coming to the pier. In 1923, an indoor playground was set up in the north shed of the passenger and freight buildings; open from 9 a.m. to 10 p.m., the playground drew nearly 173,000 visitors in 1925. But two years later, city officials were critical of a "mediocre season," in part the result of lax management. The decision was made to operate the pier again as a park field-house on the lake.

Gone were the Merry-Go-Round and Whip, their place taken by a program emphasizing uplift and education. Lectures and movies on countries of the world complemented drama and music selections while the children's theatre continued as before. Pier management was proud to report theatre performances were along "civic and patriotic lines" and constituted an "outstandingly unique civic demonstration not only of Chicago, but of the entire country." This emphasis on civic programming continued to 1940.

The pier also included one of the city's early radio stations. The station was an outgrowth of the less-than-cordial labor relations that prevailed in 1920s Chicago. Big business did not take kindly to organized labor, which returned the favor. Construction was just one of many problem industries, different only in that federal judge (and soon-to-be baseball commissioner) Kennesaw Mountain Landis was asked to arbitrate differences.

John Fitzpatrick, the president of the Chicago Federation of Labor, wanted a way to counter working-class stereotypes as well as to reach the great mass of working Chicagoans. The solution was radio. Local and state union officials were certain that, "If in man's emancipation from physical, intellectual, religious, political and economic slavery the printing press is of the first importance, radio is second. In some ways it has become the best medium for effective publicity." The federation called its station WCFL, the Voice of Labor.

The station began broadcasting at the pier from the north auditorium tower for five years, beginning in 1926. Permission was given by the administration of Mayor William E. Dever. Although a Democrat and a memeber of the tanners' union, Dever had not taken sides in the numerous labor-management disputes of the middle 1920s. With the next mayoral election just a year off, Dever probably wanted to mend fences with organized labor.

WCFL intended to "influence or educate the public mind upon the meaning and objects of trade unions and the Federation of Labor, correct wrong impressions by broadcasting the truth, and advance progressive economic ideas which when actually put into operation will benefit the masses of the nation." Listeners were treated to such varied programming as "Labor News Flashes" and "Earl Hoffman's Chez Pierre Orchestra."

The station's location also represented an important symbolic victory for the CFL. A presence on Municipal Pier connected organized labor to the Chicago Plan and suggested that the CFL possessed a civic vision equal to that of the Commercial Club. The federation furthered the notion by contracting to run dances at the pier into the 1930s. When the station moved its studios to the American Furniture Mart in 1931, the transmitter remained at the pier for another four years.

While radio broadcasting was not one of the planned uses of the pier, steamship service was. The steamers were a common sight at Municipal Pier, along with the smaller excursion boats

The east end of the pier, circa 1916. Smaller excursion boats used this section of the pier to ferry passengers to and from Lincoln and Jackson parks.

One of the lake steamers docked at the pier. Passengers often could choose between travelling to a specific vacation spot or taking a cruise.

One of the innovations of the pier was the Grand Avenue streetcar which continued onto the pier. Steamship passengers rode the streetcar to their particular gates.

View of Ogden Slip and Municipal Pier, 1922. City officials hoped to consolidate steamship traffic at the pier.

Municipal Pier in all its civic glory, 1920.

that took passengers on short trips to and from Lincoln or Jackson Park. (One of these boats, the *Favorite*, capsized during a summer storm in 1927. Twenty-seven people drowned in the accident while at least another fifty were saved through the efforts of rescuers including future movie-Tarzan Johnny Weissmuller.) The steamers as much as anything symbolized the pier during its first golden age.

The Great Lakes cruise ships were all about adventure. In a time before suburban sprawl, they could deliver passengers to a wilderness that existed just to the north on either side of Lake Michigan. All a family had to do was take the Grand Avenue streetcar that went up the pier and stopped at the various ticket offices. The Michigan Transit Company advertised the pier itself as one of the pleasures of a trip: "Open-air promenades, large, airy waiting and rest rooms, a restaurant, observation towers from which one may look far out over the broad expanse of Lake Michigan or over Chicago's wonderful, serrated sky-line—all combine to make the Municipal Pier an object of interest

and enjoyment in itself. . . ."

That was just the start. On board the *Manitou*, *Puritan* or *Missouri*, children could imagine a world of adventure on the high seas. Parents might watch the make-believe from deck chairs, adult dreams taking the form of a voyage on Cunard or the White Star Line. Or passengers may have enjoyed the seductive images of a brochure: the "sweet murmur" of waves on a distant shore; "pure, bracing air"; a beautiful landscape. These were the ingredients for "relaxation, rest, inspiration, renewed bodily strength and mental vigor—in other words a **real vacation.**"

The Goodrich Transit Company was another of the steamship lines offering service from the pier. Goodrich charged five dollars for passengers to take their cars on board for the trip to Benton Harbor in 1927. The trip to Mackinac was another popular Goodrich offering. The steamer *Carolina* sailed on five-day excursions, a full itinerary every day, even the opportunity to play deck golf. Cost in June 1928 was forty dollars round trip, meals and berth included.

The *Carolina* also took Chicago Boy Scouts to camp in Michigan.

There was a sublime magic to Municipal Pier in the 1920s. A Scout from Bridgeport could get out of a tough city neighborhood for a camp cruise across Lake Michigan. A family recently arrived from Mississippi may have beheld "Chicago's wonderful, serrated sky-line" from the pier auditorium as Bishop Archibald J. Carey called for Chicago to experience a spiritual advancement that led to brotherhood. A young couple may have taken the Grand Avenue streetcar to attend a dance. Or a group of eleven-year-olds, veterans of the Children's Civic Theatre, may have fancied themselves great actors in the mold of Douglas Fairbanks or Mary Pickford.

The pier did not revive the port of Chicago; the railroad together with the motor truck and expanding highway system crushed that dream. But the pier succeeded beyond question as a community center. Here was a place to go and enjoy a multitude of activities. An individual's poverty or boredom gave way, if only for a few hours, on a visit to Municipal Pier. Then came a series of changes.

The Great Depression was not a direct cause of the pier's decline in popularity. If anything, the Depression probably helped attendance for several years. With nearly half of the city's working population unemployed by October 1932, Chicagoans did not have much disposable income for entertainment. The pier possessed the great virtue of being free.

People exploited that advantage in May 1931 during the Chicago Jubilee. This was a week-long event promoters hoped would serve as "a distinctive civic announcement of the hopeful trend of the times." While the Jubilee did not end the Depression, it did send 200,000 people to the pier on May 21. They came to see the 659 Army Air Corps planes that flew overhead as part of the celebration.

The pier also remained popular during the summers of 1933 and 1934, when another world's fair was taking place. This was the Century of Progress, marking Chicago's 100th birthday. Visitors in July 1933 were able to watch the Italian flyer Italo Balbo land his fleet of twenty-four seaplanes to the north of the pier, or they could take a boat to the fair site at Northerly Island (later Meigs Field).

The pier even expanded its reputation in the 1930s as a center for trade shows. Heat was installed in the passenger sheds during 1936–37

so that shows could continue year-round. Other work on the pier was an unintended consequence of massive unemployment as state and federal work-relief programs focussed on pier renovation. But by decade's end it was clear the pier had lost a great deal of its popularity.

The decline in the steamship business was one indication. Passenger traffic at the pier declined from 471,000 in 1926 to 258,000 five years later. The Depression was only one reason for the falloff. Increasingly in the 1920s, steamship lines found themselves competing with trucks and automobiles. People were taken with the idea of choosing a destination for themselves, free of any schedule. In addition, as states embarked on highway construction, trucks were proving they could haul freight as cheaply as ships.

When Municipal Pier opened in 1916, there were 54,000 automobiles registered in the city. By 1932, Chicagoans owned just under 400,000. The more people drove, the more the pier became simply one of any number of destination points. And the more Chicagoans drove,

A crowd of 200,000 people watched from the pier as a flight of 659 Army Air Corps planes passed overhead on May 21, 1931. The flight was part of the Chicago Jubilee, an attempt to celebrate away the Depression.

The pier's roof garden promised "a truly Venetian scene"
at sunset. It also made an
exceptional public space
where people could eat, converse and watch the world go
by. *The collection of* David R.
Phillips

the less patient they were about places not surrounded by parking lots.

Two new forms of entertainment also drew people from the pier. The first was the movie house. By 1929, there were enough movie theatres in the city to accommodate half the population in the course of an average business day. Not only were the seats available, people wanted to go to the show.

George L. Rapp, architect of the Chicago Theater, explained the lure of a trip to the movies: "Watch the bright light in the eyes of the tired shop girl who hurries noiselessly over carpets and sighs with satisfaction as she walks amid furnishings that once delighted the hearts of queens. See the toil-worn father whose dreams have never come true, and look inside his heart as he finds strength and rest within the theater." If the movie house was not the "shrine to democracy" that Rapp claimed, it was competition for the pier. So was the radio, which did not even require people to leave their houses to be entertained. All they had to do was turn the dial and sit back as the Shadow, Ma Perkins or Fibber McGee and Molly joined them the living room.

Where the pier required effort on a visitor's part, movies and radio permitted a more passive form of entertainment; at the same time, the car was becoming a recreation activity complete unto itself. Technology was giving people new choices in spending leisure time. Too often, decisions came at the expense of the pier. Chicagoans were forgetting how to use a civic treasure. They would not remember for close to forty years.

In December 1927, the city council decided on a name change for Municipal Pier. It would now be known as Navy Pier, in honor of those Chicagoans and Midwesterners who served in the Navy during World War I. The change was prophetic. In August 1941, on the eve of a second world war, the United States Navy began operating the pier as a military facility.

From Training School to University 4

The Second World War transformed the United States, particularly its second largest city. Scrap and bond drives, food and gasoline rationing, Civilian Defense drills and Victory gardens, all these became part of everyday life in Chicago, 1941-45. So did the gold star, hung in a window to announce that someone in that house or apartment had made the ultimate sacrifice.

Going into the war, Franklin Roosevelt wanted to transform the U.S. economy into an "arsenal of democracy" to defeat the enemy. Industrial Chicago proved equal to the task. Between 1940 and the war's end, some $1.3 billion was poured into factory construction; that plant expansion coupled with military contracts helped contribute 438,000 new jobs to the city economy.

If Chicago did not make everything for the war, it came close. Fifty area companies manufactured parts for the B-29 bomber. The Chicago Roller Skate Company converted from making play equipment to the manufacture of nose sections for bombers. And Rock-Ola, famous for its jukeboxes, switched over to rifle production.

With so much manpower and equipment on hand, the Chicago area made yet another contribution to the war effort, as a training center. Glenview Naval Air Station, Great Lakes Naval Training Center and Fort Sheridan all operated close to the city; Great Lakes and Fort Sheridan combined to train over 1.4 million recruits. Training also took part in the city proper. The Board of Education made available some of its property, including Chicago Vocational School, for military training while several universities also trained military personnel. And then there was Navy Pier.

The Navy took over the pier in the summer of 1941 for a naval aviation ground training school for mechanics. The pier was to accommodate ten thousand sailors and marines, including space for barracks. The pier's new role meant considerable construction. A drill hall and a hangar building were erected just north and south of the head house, respectively; an auxiliary mess hall went up between the freight and passenger sheds just west of the terminal building; and the open-air shelter building was bricked over to become both mess hall and galley. Men slept in the upper portion of the sheds and trained in the lower.

The Navy operated various training programs at the pier throughout the war. Those enrolled might become aviation machinist's mates, metal smiths or diesel engine technicians. By the time training ceased in July 1946, some sixty thousand people—including sailors from Great Britain, Canada, Brazil and Peru—were trained at the pier.

Among them was Chester Schneider, who graduated from his training course on Navy Pier in January 1944. A native New Yorker, Schneider had no problem acclimating himself to piers and subways; if anything, Chicago was a small city to him. But life on the pier did take some getting used to, starting with the six a.m. reveille provided by a drum and bugle corps that marched down the open area between the freight and passenger sheds. "You wouldn't believe the vibrations of that steel-beamed, corrugated metal structure that the blare of bugles and the beating of drums could evoke," Schneider recalled in a 1991 interview.

There was also the challenge of dealing with birds. The sparrows that roosted in the living quarters showed little respect for military notions of cleanliness. While the sea gulls were content to stay outside, they insisted on offering their own version of taps, or lights-out, at nine p.m. The bugle was followed by "a unified screeching and singing" to remind the Navy that the gulls would be the ones to decide when recruits would go to sleep.

In addition, training included a good deal of marching from class to class. For fun, classes liked to march as close to an oncoming group as possible without causing harm; Schneider "learned quickly to lean my right shoulder out to brush against every man in a passing column, especially if it was a Marine group." Constant marching upset the wooden paving blocks in the middle section of the pier, which in turn meant the periodic appearance of a "large tar

Navy Pier trained sixty thousand American and Allied naval personnel during World War II. *National Archives* (facing page)

37

boiler." The boiler provided "a ready supply of molten tar" used for keeping the blocks in place.

Sometimes, the work crews operated the boiler on days when the men were ordered to air out their bedding. The inevitable smell of tar picked up by the bedding was one of the smells Schneider associated with the pier. Another was apricots: "Stewed apricots, apricot pie or even fresh apricots; count on them, they were served at each meal." On a trip to Navy Pier forty-three years later, Chester Schneider could still smell apricots.

A small portion of the pier was reserved for a tugboat and barge charged with the job of retrieving Navy planes that had crashed into Lake Michigan. These accidents were not totally unexpected. Rather, they were a by-product of one of the most fascinating training efforts of the war. Anybody who passed Navy Pier in 1944 or 1945 could tell that some serious military activity was going on just by looking at the two aircraft carriers moored to the south of the pier.

The war in the Pacific often consisted of naval engagements involving carrier-based aircraft. Training a steady flow of pilots was essential, but taking a carrier out of active service for that purpose was out of the question. The balance of power in the first half of the war with Japan was so precarious the Navy could ill-afford the loss of a carrier, even for training. Then, in early 1942, an officer stationed at Great Lakes proposed a solution—train flyers on Lake Michigan.

Commander Richard F. Whitehead argued that lake-based training would free the Navy from worry of attack or the presence of mines. The only drawback was that aircraft carriers did not ordinarily ply the Great Lakes. Anticipating this problem, Commander Whitehead con-

vinced his superiors that the training could be done on lake steamers converted for the purpose.

The boats chosen were both side paddle-wheel steamers, the *Seeandbee* (named for the owners, the Cleveland and Buffalo Transit Company) and the *Greater Buffalo*. The *Seeandbee* was purchased and converted first; it was commissioned the USS *Wolverine* in August 1942. The *Greater Buffalo* followed as the USS *Sable* nine months later.

The *Seeandbee*, constructed in 1912, was the largest side paddle-wheel steamer in the world, with a length of approximately five hundred feet; the overhang on the flight deck added another fifty feet to the ship. The *Greater Buffalo*, built in 1923, was slightly longer. In contrast, carriers like the *Enterprise* and *Yorktown* were some three hundred feet longer, a distance which gave a margin of safety for planes landing or taking off. But pilots learned to make do, just as they did with another feature of the two lake carriers. The landing decks were only twenty-six feet above water. An aircraft taking off any carrier tends to dip downward as it leaves the deck. The challenge on *Wolverine* and *Sable* was to make sure the dip did not turn into a splash.

The two carriers presented a unique sight during the war years. The *Wolverine* could be identified by the four smokestacks coming out of its bridge; the *Sable* had two stacks. Even after their conversion, both ships were propelled by their side paddle-wheels. Early on, the *Wolverine* sported a second distinguishing feature: The smokestacks belched out a heavy smoke that made landing nearly impossible. The problem was caused by an engine-room crew unfamiliar with the furnaces, which burned best when coal was placed further in. Experience, coupled with

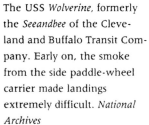

The USS *Wolverine*, formerly the *Seeandbee* of the Cleveland and Buffalo Transit Company. Early on, the smoke from the side paddle-wheel carrier made landings extremely difficult. *National Archives*

When the public was allowed on the pier in November 1944, people saw the types of landing craft used in invasions. *National Archives*

a more suitable grade of coal, cleared visibility around the *Wolverine.*

Weather proved to be another challenge. The Navy found it could attempt year-round operations, ice permitting, but winter training was not easy. A snowstorm in the winter of 1943 led to the loss of three planes without a trace. Such hazards as wind and ice demanded total concentration in spite of personal discomfort. In the words of former president George Bush, "I remember those Great Lake flights very well in the open cockpit that winter. Coldest I ever was in my life." But he qualified.

The *Wolverine* and *Sable* worked around the constraints of the particular day and season to maximize the number of planes handled. The carriers worked only in daylight and spent the day steaming into the wind so as to give pilots optimum conditions. The planes, meanwhile, took off from Glenview Naval Air Station. Pilots like George Bush, who remembers "concentrating on this major step," may have had different priorities than the civilians who lived along their flight paths. Some Evanston residents complained that planes flew so low they were stripping the leaves from trees.

Pilots qualified as carrier-ready when they completed eight landings and takeoffs from the *Wolverine* or *Sable;* in late 1944 the requirement was raised to fourteen. No matter how exciting

or frightening that first landing was, the pilot had to be ready to take off again almost immediately. The carrier decks could only handle two or three aircraft at a time, and the ships were not equipped with elevators to store planes below deck. Although flight-deck accidents were common enough, none of the twenty-one pilots killed in training died during shipboard operations. Over 250 planes were lost in Lake Michigan.

An October 1943 story in the *Tribune* recounted what to that point had been the worst day ever for the *Wolverine.* In one inci-

Crew members of the *Sable* working on a plane. Neither the *Sable* nor *Wolverine* had storage capacity below decks, so it was imperative to keep the landing deck clear. *National Archives*

A Grumman Wildcat, 1944.
Damaged planes were
unloaded on the pier.
National Archives

The *Wolverine* and *Sable* and
Sable moored just south of
Navy Pier, sometime in the
1940s. Both ships were
scrapped in 1948.

dent, a plane was "apparently headed for a sat-
isfactory landing. The tail hook engaged the first
cable—and then things happened! The cable
seemed to yield. T-8 [the training plane, a torpe-
do-bomber] careened wildly over to port [the
left side], and seamen's heads disappeared like
magic into the safety shelters beside the cat-
walk."

The *Wolverine* immediately changed course
to keep the wind from blowing the plane over-
board. Luckily, the pilot—"a slight kid of about
20 with big ears and brown hair"—was not
seriously hurt; a support craft ferried the plane
back to Navy Pier. Later that day, a second plane
was involved in a landing mishap. A Grumman
Wildcat made a bad approach and was waved

This Dauntless dive bomber was retrieved fourteen miles out into Lake Michigan in October 1990. The plane had been involved in a landing mishap on the *Wolverine* November 23, 1943. The pilot escaped injury. *National Archives*

off, but it was too late: "Before anyone could blink the plane had struck on its right wing and was in the water off the starboard bow."

The plane "sank a split second after the *Wolverine*'s stern passed the spot. The pilot went down with his plane, but in a moment bobbed up again, supported by his Mae West [life jacket]. Seconds later, he was rescued by the crash boat." Ironically, modern salvage techniques have made the crash sites an important source for the now-rare planes.

The *Wolverine* and *Sable* sailed out of Chicago seven days a week in what seemed a never-ending training program. May 21, 1943, was both the *Sable*'s first day of operation and its busiest. Fifty-nine pilots qualified as the carrier recorded the equivalent of a landing a minute for nine straight hours. The *Wolverine* did even better, recording 633 landings in early June 1944. By war's end, the two carriers qualified nearly eighteen thousand pilots and twenty-two thousand carrier-support personnel.

With the surrender of Japan in August 1945, the two side paddle-wheel carriers were moored next to Navy Pier. They were decommissioned that November, sold for scrap, and broken up in 1948. The pier, however, experienced a different fate as Chicagoans prepared for the post-war world.

No one knew how well reconversion of the economy to peacetime would work. A severe recession followed World War I, and some observers even feared a return of the Great Depression. In response, Chicago businessmen pressured the Navy into moving out of the pier in time for the 1946 convention season. Promoters were planning to book four large trade shows that promised to generate $90 million for the city. The Navy agreed, but the pier soon found itself with a new tenant who promised not to get in the way of trade exhibits, stevedores or teamsters. For the next eighteen years, Navy Pier would be Harvard on the Rocks, a two-year campus for the University of Illinois.

The war changed the way returning veterans viewed themselves. They had risked death and seen the world. They would gladly return home, but not necessarily to the old life they had once known. One GI explained, "Take these kids from the hills, the service opened their eyes some. . . . And some of these guys from Chicago, why they'd never been outside of Chicago. They talked about fellows 'from the sticks' and they'd never been out in the 'sticks'—they'd never known what the 'sticks' were."

The Servicemen's Readjustment Act of 1944, or GI Bill, offered a way to focus this change, through education. The act provided liberal education benefits for returning veterans. Suddenly, the idea of a college education for the masses went from dream to possibility.

By November 1947, over seventy-five thousand veterans were enrolled in Illinois colleges and universities. University of Chicago president Robert M. Hutchins predicted the GI Bill

Student parking at the pier was a perennial problem. This may explain why parking tickets were payable to the traffic violations bureau of the Municipal Court, also located at Navy Pier. *Alumni Association University of Illinois at Chicago*

The "joys" of registration at Navy Pier. *Alumni Association University of Illinois at Chicago*

"Of course, it's a little hard to swim out to it, but I never have to worry about a parking space."

42

would transform college campuses into hobo jungles, but these new students were entirely serious about their educations. In fact, they were serious to the point of overwhelming existing facilities. The University of Illinois alone had eleven thousand vets on its Urbana campus; that figure represented sixty-five percent of the school's prewar enrollment. A satellite campus in Chicago soon became necessary as a way to alleviate overcrowding downstate.

And what a campus Navy Pier was, the only one in the world on which lecture halls, classrooms and labs jutted three thousand feet into a lake. Since the Navy already had transformed the pier into a training school, it made sense to continue its educational function, only now on an undergraduate level. The first step in establishing a campus was completed when Mayor Ed Kelly assured nervous convention businesspeople that only surplus space on the pier would be used. The University of Illinois then leased the lower level, north side of the pier along with the terminal building and auditorium.

An auxiliary structure erected by the Navy west of the terminal building became classrooms. The galley, located in a bricked-over section of the shelter building, became the university cafeteria while the mess hall—also in the shelter building—was transformed into the library. (As to lockers, some students found

theirs in what had once been the brig.) The auditorium doubled as university assembly hall and women's gym. The men's gymnasium was located in the old Navy drill hall, built during the war just southwest of the pier. This gym was big enough to fit three full-sized basketball courts as well as eight classes simultaneously.

Classes began in October 1946 for what was a two-year program, after which students transferred to other institutions. The student body reached slightly over forty-five hundred in

1947 and then hovered around four thousand. In some ways Navy Pier was the typical college campus. Students could join the Chi-Illini Chemistry Club, the Dance Band or French Club, and there was a school football team, although for obvious reasons practice and home games could not take place on campus. Out-of-bounds simply would have been too risky.

The new school's administration emphasized that the pier was a legitimate institution in every way, only narrower. A promotional pamphlet—Why Is The University of Illinois At Navy Pier?—outlined the decision. Overcrowding downstate, the success of the GI Bill, the large number of Chicago-area students and cost considerations for those students all made Navy Pier a logical choice. And since the pier had been operated as a school by the Navy, the university decided on a bit of continuity, with a navy man to serve as dean of the undergraduate division. The new dean, Captain Charles Caveny, had been the executive and education officer on the pier during the war.

The university also may have felt the need to define higher education to students who had little idea what it entailed. The 1920s' stereotype of college as much party and little work did not apply. The university outlined its objectives as:

1. To educate the student.
2. To guide the passage of its students into adult life.
3. To meet the needs of the students over the breadth of their psychological natures.
4. To extend and disseminate knowledge.
5. To prepare the student to accept responsibilities.
6. To foster good human relationships.

The "educational, social and cultural programs" at Navy Pier would provide students with the same educational experience that "has been so long a part of University of Illinois tradition." The veterans of Guadalcanal and D-Day expected no less.

But what made this University of Illinois campus memorable had little to do with any resemblance to downstate Urbana. It was the "pier" part, such as phys. ed. electives that offered fishing and swimming on and in Lake Michigan. For the more than 100,000 students who attended Navy Pier from 1946 to 1964, school was rarely ordinary.

One of the basic challenges college students have always faced is getting from one class to

Like other commuter schools, students at Navy Pier struggled to find a sense of community. The dance band helped.
Alumni Association University of Illinois at Chicago

During World War II the mess hall fed sailors assigned to Navy Pier. After the war the space was converted into the university library.

The auditorium at the east end of the pier was used as the women's gymnasium.
Alumni Association University of Illinois at Chicago 43

Frank Lloyd Wright with architecture students at the pier, sometime in the late 1940s or early 1950s. When the pier opened in 1916, Wright already had established a national reputation as an architect.

An engineering class at the pier. Classroom windows facing the water periodically let in errant lines of rope from ships. Interior classrooms offered a different surprise—truckers sometimes poked their heads in through a window to ask for directions.
Alumni Association University of Illinois at Chicago

44

another, with too many books and not enough time. Navy Pier was not a huge campus, just very long with hallways very cramped. Ed Smason, who attended the pier in the late 1940s, recalled, "The endless tunnel-like corridor, interrupted by a bullet-straight row of tree-size pillars, kept you snuggled together on those 10-minute snake crawls between classes."

Getting to a few areas in particular was even worse: "If that traffic crawled, it shuffled in the low-ceiling hallway of the newer second floor classroom area near the rear of the Pier." There was a potential upside, however. "You couldn't help but get acquainted if you would shout above the babble."

Once in class, students had no guarantee they could keep the weather out. Student Dave Manthey remembered that, "Only at the Pier could a geography class be threatened by a storm." Bad weather on Lake Michigan meant "water would seep under the thin north wall at the back of the classroom." If nothing else, the experience helped students understand life in Holland. The wind and waves also attacked walls by pushing driftwood against the pier. In one instance, driftwood battered down a plywood wall in the English Department. A flood ensued.

School at the pier was never unremittingly dull, not when a seaplane sank just beyond the library windows or a line from a docking ship sailed through an open classroom window. Anything could happen on campus, even a visit by Frank Lloyd Wright or the comedy team of Martin and Lewis, so it made sense to pay attention.

Other oddities marked learning and teaching on the pier. The ventilation system introduced a new generation of students to visits from birds—and bats. Trucks were another interruption. They were constantly moving on or off the pier, and sometimes drivers became lost. Without any gas stations nearby, a classroom was the only place to get directions.

The washrooms also required some understanding early on. English professor Laurette Kirstein found that Navy terminology had not been translated into civilian vernacular: "One of the big problems we encountered in the first year was trying to figure out whether Head 1 was for men and Head 2 for women or vice versa." And, like everyone else, Professor Kirstein learned that it paid to expect the unexpected in class. While teaching one day, she noticed her students were giggling. "I looked up behind me and saw the legs of a man in overalls dangling from the ventilating shaft above. Eventually, he disappeared, apparently to go somewhere else to disrupt someone else's class."

There were at least two advantages to attending school on Navy Pier. Anyone who wanted to catch smelt in season would have been hard-pressed to find a better spot for fishing. And for those who were able to gain access, the trade shows promised numerous delights. One student went so far as to place a box at an exit, with a sign directing convention-goers to dispose of their badges accordingly. The badges were then recycled for student and faculty use. Among the conventions worth "crashing" were the Restaurant Show (free samples) and the Household Show (merchandise at half-price on the last day).

The *Illinois Alumni News* in a September 1956 issue expressed the sentiments of those who were a part of this Harvard on the Rocks. "Navy Pier has been a godsend," an editorial noted, "but it never was intended to be a university." The pier had always been thought of by officials as a temporary facility, possibly to be phased out after the surge of GI Bill students subsided. But when the veterans moved on, administrators discovered a mass of Chicago-area students who wanted to attend school locally.

After a detailed search, the university chose a permanent location on Taylor Street, slightly south and west of downtown. The new campus was ready in February 1965. The idea of a Chicago-based public university, which dated to the 1860s, had become reality. Bernard Kogan was one of the faculty members who made the move from the pier to the new campus. An English professor and author of a history of the pier, Professor Kogan understood he was part

There were none of the usual Gothic trappings about the Navy Pier campus; it was a utilitarian environment throughout. This is the student lounge at the west end of the pier. *Alumni Association University of Illinois at Chicago*

Sometimes, when the weather was right and exams were out of the way, the pier must have felt like any other school. *Alumni Association University of Illinois at Chicago*

of something special: "The immediate feeling was one of excitement and anticipation. There was a sense of being in on history."

History already had been made at the University of Illinois, Navy Pier. Three journalists were among the 100,000 students who attended the pier; their assessments of the school mirror the experiences of classmates. Army veteran John Chancellor described the attitude of the 1940s' students as "a lot of fanatic vets on roller skates." Chancellor entered school in 1947. "We had 10 minutes between classes and half a mile of classrooms laid end to end," a distance some students tried to cover on skates.

Students rushed about in more than the literal sense: "Everybody was in a hurry. We'd

45

all lost a couple years of our lives and wanted
to make them up," Chancellor said in a 1991
interview. "And it was serious scholarship. We
were steely-eyed sons of bitches. . . . There was
that sense of having to hustle, to make up time.
Learn as much as you could—and get out in the
world." That education and sense of urgency
helped propel Chancellor to a long career as a
journalist for NBC News.

Bernard Shaw of CNN attended in the 1960s.
He recalled, "The most memorable thing about
Navy Pier, and the most awful thing about it,
was getting off that trolley bus at the turn-
around circle across from the front entrance,
being late for class and having to be a decathlon
champion [and] run those halls to get to the

other end of the Pier." However daunting,
Shaw found the experience worthwhile. "I
wouldn't want to replace that by having gone
to school on a campus of lush greenness. It's
part of my chemistry and part of my makeup."

William Braden of the Chicago *Sun-Times*
noted that, "At Navy Pier, in the shoals of aca-
deme, the message appropriately was: Shape
up or ship out." It was not easy. "Students swel-
tered in summer and froze in winter. But they
survived, and thrived." The success of Navy Pier
as a school was measured less by classroom size
or campus amenities than by the testament of
its students.

In 1955, about midway through the pier's
incarnation as university campus, Richard J.
Daley became mayor. Daley saw Navy Pier as
a facility to help maintain Chicago's economic
base. When circumstances proved otherwise,
Daley refused to abandon the pier. He sought
out new uses and, in so doing, found that the
pier's future could reflect the civic fuction from
its past.

Shifting Roles

5

Everything old was new again. So it seemed to Chicago's civic boosters by the end of the 1950s. They had embraced yet another transportation project dating to the French explorers, and they again hoped to make Chicago a world-class port. There was even a proposal for another canal, this one of extraordinary dimensions. And many of the hopes focused on Navy Pier.

The latest project was the St. Lawrence Seaway, an idea born in the time of Jacques Cartier in the 1530s. The seaway, constructed and operated jointly by the United States and Canada, opened the Great Lakes to ocean traffic. Work on the billion-dollar venture took five years, beginning in 1954. The first ship to dock at the pier via the seaway was a Dutch freighter, the *Johan Willem Friso*, in April 1959. Chicago was now ready for the commercial "manifest destiny" that J. Paul Goode had predicted in 1909.

William Clark took up the theme in a *Chicago Sunday Tribune Magazine* article, June 2, 1959. The seaway's opening meant nothing less than "The World's Greatest City Is Being Born." Clark believed that world trade would show that "Chicago undeniably is at the threshold of a new golden era which will make achievements of the last 100 years seem pale indeed by comparison."

The canal fever of the nineteenth century had returned in St. Lawrence form, along with a dash of romance. No expectation was too great. Chicago would receive up to a thousand ships a year within fifteen years of the seaway's opening. Industry and agriculture would expand, shipbuilding would become a major industry and, in all, 890,000 new jobs would be created. Few critics were inclined to disagree with the assessment of writer Paul Kunning, who predicted a future in which Chicago emerged as "the greatest inland port in the world."

One observer was so convinced of the benefits Chicago would derive from the St. Lawrence Seaway that he proposed a canal not unlike the one Alfred Beirly proposed in 1908. But Beirly's "plan of tremendous scope" measured only several miles long and no more than seven hun-

dred feet wide. U. A. Sanabria envisioned a canal across the length of southern Michigan to connect Chicago with Lake Erie. Sanabria argued that his plan would reduce the travel distance to Chicago by six hundred miles, increase trade among Western nations and strike a blow at communism all at the same time. "We must face the fact that if our free Western world is to triumph over the Soviet system," Sanabria counseled, "we must win the Cold War of creating business."

The *Daily News* offered readers a different dream: using the St. Lawrence "to hop a ship in Chicago and enjoy a pleasure cruise to Europe. Or you'll ride as far as Toronto, Mon-

Navy Pier may have been one of the few places in Chicago untouched by railroads. That changed in July 1956 when freight service was extended in part of the effort to ready the pier for the opening of the St. Lawrence Seaway.

(*From left*) Queen Elizabeth II, Illinois Governor William G. Stratton, Mayor Daley and Prince Philip make their way to Navy Pier to visit the International Trade Fair in July 1959. Big Bill Thompson might have treated the appearance of royalty in different fashion.

An opening-day crowd at the trade fair. The St. Lawrence Seaway promised to bring goods from around the world to Chicago consumers.

treal or Quebec—and the service will be strictly first-class." That the Cunard Line might never service Chicago with a fleet of ocean liners didn't really matter. With twenty-six foreign shipping lines using the pier in 1959, promoters for the Chicago International Trade Fair expected Navy Pier to be "favored by its central location over other facilities for the rapidly developing passenger traffic."

Some if not all the hopes attached to the seaway had a basis in fact. Chicago had long benefited from its air, rail and highway links; that network could be used in turn to strengthen the city as a port facility. To insure that it did, Richard J. Daley began updating Navy Pier in 1956. Railroad lines finally were extended onto the pier proper, and its south side was expanded with a concrete dock addition measuring 96 by 1,100 feet. These improvements thus allowed ships to unload large cargoes that the pier had not been designed to handle.

Richard Daley became mayor at a time when cities across the United States had entered into a state of serious decline. Chicago was not immune. It too lost a substantial portion of its industrial and middle-class tax base, though not to the extent of St. Louis, Detroit or other cities. Daley was able to fight a holding action by promoting economic development through public works and cooperation with the private sector, which in turn generated favorable publicity nationwide. Chicago was, as *Newsweek* reported, "a major American city that actually works." Trains ran on time and garbage workers did not go out on strike. And in summer of 1959, Chicago's Navy Pier was the place that royalty visited.

The International Trade Fair at the pier that July coincided with the official opening of the St. Lawrence Seaway. Not only did crowds of Chicagoans flock again to the pier, there was also a special guest, Queen Elizabeth II of England. From an historical viewpoint, the trip was filled with irony. When he was campaigning for a third term as mayor in 1927, Big Bill Thompson announced he would be "handing the king one on the snoot" if George V came to town. This time, Chicagoans were downright enthusiastic about the presence of British royalty.

The queen, her husband Prince Philip and their entourage made a whirlwind, thirty-one minute tour of Navy Pier in electric carts. They stopped to receive a brocade sari and bolt of raw silk from the Indian pavilion; greet Ceylon's national dancers; and hear a Marine chorus sing "Auld Lang Syne." The queen found exhibits to be "frightfully impressive" and "frightfully exciting." Upon seeing a Rolls Royce on display, Prince Philip kidded onlookers to keep a respectful distance from what he called "the best car in the show."

There were at least two occasions for the Navy Pier crowd to express itself. At one stop, Chicago carpenter Arthur Loughran managed to get through police lines and strike up a conversation with Prince Philip; the prince told the Dublin immigrant—who had married an English nurse—to "have a Guinness [ale] on me" if he visited England. And when the queen and her party finished their tour, George Gray of Oak Park saw them off with music from his Scottish bagpipes.

The International Trade Fair itself was the Pageant of Progress gone global. The sixteen-day-long event featured entertainment and exhibits from sixty-five nations. At its conclusion, the fair functioned as a true bazaar when many of the participating nations put the goods from their exhibits up for sale. Anyone from the South or West Side had the opportunity to be Marco Polo for a day while buying items from Morocco, the Republic of China or the United Arab Republic.

Among the exhibitors was IBM, which displayed its 305 Ramac computer—or "electronic brain" in the words of a *Tribune* story. The computer welcomed the mayor to the fair and informed his son William that the most important event of 1948 (the year of William Daley's birth) was the Chicago Railroad Fair. Just under 850,000 people visited the trade fair.

The first half of the new decade looked bright for the pier. Cargo sheds were constructed, and the concrete dock addition on the pier's south side was extended to 2,400 feet total; the new construction together with dredging of the area just to the south gave the pier six berths for ocean-going vessels. And the anticipated move of the University of Illinois off the pier to its west-side campus would make yet more space available for shipping.

As the 1960s began, it appeared that international trade indeed would make the Chicago economy boom as it had during the 1920s and World War II. And few could disagree that Navy Pier had played a key role. "Chicago's speedy construction of berth and cargo facilities for ocean-going vessels at Navy Pier has trans-

formed this forty-seven-year old landmark, long regarded as something of a shabby white elephant, into a thriving center for world commerce," the *Tribune* wrote in 1961. There was little reason to think it would not continue.

Evidence to the contrary came soon enough. In late 1963 a group of investors proposed constructing a 920-foot "sky tower" at the east end of Navy Pier. Patterned after the Space Needle at the Seattle World's Fair, the structure was to be built at an estimated cost of $12 million. The proposal was typical of the time, a massive project to announce that news of this particular city's demise had been premature. And like other urban renewal plans of the 1960s, this one threatened a city landmark. A project spokesman noted that the pier's "auditorium would have to be eliminated" to make room for the tower.

The idea then was changed to locate the tower at the foot of the pier, but promoters abandoned the project in part over concerns that it would interfere with landing approaches at Meigs Field. However, the land west of the pier was again the subject of controversy in 1965

when developers announced plans for the construction of an apartment building, Lake Point Tower. Lakefront preservationists objected that construction would lead to overbuilding in the area. Although the apartment tower was built, the protests contributed to the passage of a lakefront protection ordinance by the city council in 1973. Thus, residents of Lake Point Tower were assured a stunning view of Lake Michigan while Navy Pier was given one—and only one—highrise neighbor east of Lake Shore Drive.

If the pier had remained busy as a port facility, the development controversies probably would never have arisen. The two tower proposals were a sign that things were not quite right. By the late 1960s, the pier was in an obvious state of commercial decline. The problem was related to the St. Lawrence Seaway, which had never generated the level of international trade expected. There was steady traffic, but not enough to keep both Navy Pier and the more modern facilities at Lake Calumet busy. More than two-hundred-fifty ocean-going ships a year anchored at the pier in the mid-1960s; by 1974, only twenty freighters docked

The construction of Lake Point Tower in 1968 offered a contrast in architectural styles on the lakefront: a contemporary work in the spirit of Mies van der Rohe rising above the Beaux-Arts outline of Navy Pier.

Following the success of the Space Needle at the Seattle World's Fair, a Chicago corporation announced plans to build a 965-foot tall tower on the east end of Navy Pier. The project later was to be located just west of the pier, where Lake Point Tower now stands. *Chicago Sun-Times*

(*Facing page*)Preparation for the International Trade Fair included a facelift for the auditorium towers. Featured is the civic symbol that shows the two branches of the Chicago River and represents the "I Will" spirit of Chicago.

51

at the pier. Once again, Daniel Burnham was proven right: The Chicago lakefront did not need to be given over to commerce.

The falloff in traffic did offer at least one benefit. In August 1969, a Scottish freighter docked at the pier dumped as much as one thousand gallons of oil into Lake Michigan. With concern growing over pollution in the Great Lakes, a busy port operation at Navy Pier no longer seemed like such a good idea.

But what to do with the pier? As early as 1964, Richard Daley proposed redevelopment. The need for immediate action, however, was postponed when a fire destroyed the city's new convention and trade center in January 1967. McCormick Place had opened on the lakefront at Twenty-third Street in 1961 as Chicago's premier convention space. The idea was to stage shows in a modern environment rather than in such generally outdated facilities as Navy Pier, the International Amphitheatre or the Coliseum. With the fire, shows returned to the pier. But this renewed activity lasted only until the second McCormick Place opened in 1971.

The status of the pier remained in limbo until the city began planning for the upcoming

A busy Navy Pier in the summer of 1961. The south end of the pier was extended to handle large cargoes from ocean-going ships.

Bicentennial in 1976. As communities nation-wide did likewise, many were making an unpleasant discovery. The automobile had allowed Americans to escape to the suburbs after 1945, but at a price. These new places lacked a civic center, or soul, to stage so grand a celebration as a two hundredth birthday. Chicago suffered from no such drawback. The city possessed any number of sites where people could gather and celebrate. Navy Pier was one of them.

First, though, the pier needed extensive

The deterioration of Navy Pier was so advanced both inside and outside that the city could no longer ignore it in 1974. Renovation coincided with plans for the Bicentennial celebration. Shown here is the pier auditorium before restoration.
Jerome Butler

work inside and out. Since at least the 1940s, the pier had been subjected to piecemeal remodelings and deferred maintenance. To the Navy and University of Illinois, the pier had been little more than a temporary home; later, anything not related to the pier's function as a port facility was generally allowed to deteriorate. By the early 1970s, roofs, masonry and concrete were a problem throughout, and the auditorium required special attention. The interior of this grand space was exposed to the elements of Chicago's lakefront.

The city began restoration work in April 1974 under the direction of City Architect Jerome R. Butler (FAIA), an alum of the University of Illinois at Navy Pier. The auditorium and other buildings were restored while a promenade opened on the north side of the pier. Activity continued into 1975 with landscaping and further restoration as well as a solar energy project to heat the pier's east end buildings. The American Institute of Architects gave Butler a National Honor Award for his restoration of the pier's east end.

The pier performed as the Daley administration hoped it would. The program schedule that Bicentennial summer featured an international trade exposition and lakefront festival; amusement rides; entertainment; and cultural exhibits, including, fittingly, two on Chicago architecture. When fireworks filled the sky over Navy Pier that July Fourth, onlookers enjoyed the kind of civic experience that Daniel Burnham had planned for Chicago's lakefront.

In August, visitors swarmed the pier to see the Norwegian sailing ship, the *Christian Radich*, one of the more than two hundred "tall ships" that had gathered to celebrate the Fourth of July in New York harbor. In just four days, some 100,000 people viewed the 238-foot long, three-masted vessel. By summer's end, people had rediscovered what had once been common knowledge in the 1920s: Chicago's municipal pier could be the site of sublime pleasures.

Colonel Jack Riley, special events director for Mayor Daley, was one of those impressed with the public's reaction to the pier. Riley wanted the city to continue development so the pier "might just be around for the Tricentennial." The challenge, though, remained. Someone had to define what constituted the best use of the pier even as it was declared a city landmark in 1977.

Was it as a marina for four hundred sailboats

The pier auditorium with renovated brick facade and the original ribbed lighting design on the interior. Renovation work won an AIA National Honor Award for city architect Jerome R. Butler.
Jerome Butler

with a 135-acre landfill next to the new filtration plant just to the north of the pier, as suggested by Harry Weese, a prominent architect? This scheme would have created one of the offshore islands proposed by Daniel Burnham in the Chicago Plan. Or was the pier a better venue for art and culture? This was the focus the city took with its Summer of '77, using the auditorium for ballet, classical music and theater. Or should the city abandon redevelopment efforts and sell the pier to a developer who might erect housing where Navy recruits once marched? City hall did not lack for proposals.

Part of the answer became obvious in the summer of 1978, when the city scheduled its first ChicagoFest. There was nothing new in combining food and entertainment on the pier; the mix had existed since the pier's opening. What had changed was that the Bicentennial had introduced a new generation of people to the pier. This group, comprising both Chicagoans and suburbanites, immediately took to the idea of a lakefront festival at the pier. A half-million people attended, and for the next four years "ChicagoFest" and "Navy Pier" were virtually inseparable.

ChicagoFest combined elements of carnival, music fest and picnic. While it lacked the mud of Woodstock, the festival more than held its own in terms of crowds, as when 120,000 people jammed the pier on the last day of ChicagoFest 1979. And the food was probably better, or at least available in greater quantities. Visitors at the first ChicagoFest consumed 4,509 half-barrels of beer along with 62,000 pounds of meat and poultry.

Entertainment ran the gamut at ChicagoFest. Among the rock acts performing were Chuck Berry, Cheap Trick and Journey. Blues greats Willie Dixon and Muddy Waters entertained the crowds, as did jazzman Dave Bru-

The Norwegian sailing ship *Christian Radich* visited Chicago a month after participating as one of the more than two hundred "tall ships" in New York harbor for the Bicentennial. Activities during the summer of 1976 introduced the pier to a new generation of residents. *Hedrich-Blessing*

beck. And it was only appropriate for a Chicago festival to have someone sing the city's signature song. Frank Sinatra drew 25,000 people for his concert at the 1982 ChicagoFest.

It was obvious that Chicago was more than just Sinatra's kind of town. By attracting so many people, especially young suburbanites, ChicagoFest served as a three-dimensional ad campaign for city tourism. But at times ChicagoFest proved too much of a good thing. Parking and transportation were a problem, and Navy Pier strained to accommodate the crowds. Both the pier's utilities and sewage system proved inadequate to the demands of festgoers. So ChicagoFest further re-established the pier as a popular destination point as it demonstrated the need for the pier's renovation and a decision on its best use.

Any redevelopment of the pier required a mayor with the political expertise to carry it off. Taxpayers and the state government would have to be convinced as would the business community, which feared that commercial development on the pier might compete with the retail trade on north Michigan Avenue. Richard J. Daley, who had the tenure and the political support necessary for the task, died in December 1976. However, his successor, Michael A. Bilandic, did show considerable interest in the pier; the first ChicagoFest was a product of the Bilandic administration.

But Bilandic suffered the misfortune of being mayor during the infamous winter of 1978–79, when Chicago was blanketed with ninety inches of snow. With all forms of transportation difficult and at times impossible, for a time "the city that worked" appeared not to. Voters took out their frustrations in the Democratic mayoral primary. In April 1979, Jane Byrne was elected the first woman mayor in Chicago history.

Jane Byrne had a way of keeping critics off balance by utilizing the qualities of two of her predecessors. As a member of the Daley cabinet, Bryne had learned the importance of projecting the image of Chicago as the city that worked. Byrne also had a bit of Big Bill Thompson in her. She appealed to the masses as an outsider, and she depended on the grand gesture as a proof of ability; Thompson had done the same a half-century before. With Navy Pier, the new mayor showed both her Daley and Thompson selves.

Byrne saw the popularity of ChicagoFest as proof that the pier should be geared to broad appeal. In 1980, she made a tour of Baltimore and Philadelphia with officials of the Rouse Company, a Columbia, Maryland, developer. The Rouse Company already had Faneuil Hall in Boston and Harborplace in Baltimore to its credit. Basically, these projects consisted of historic sites turned into a blend of entertainment

The Legendary singer Frank Sinatra entertained thousands of people on a beautiful Chicago summer night leading everyone in singing "My Kind of Town, Chicago Is . . . . ." *Chicago Sun-Times*

and retail space. Rouse estimated that a similar plan for Navy Pier could attract sixteen million visitors a year, on the same scale as Disney World.

In 1982, the city and Rouse agreed on a $277 million redevelopment of the pier. The plan featured shops, entertainment, a 450-room hotel and 2,500-car parking garage. In addition, there was to be an art center, maritime museum, 400-slip marina and public transportation to the pier. Although the city council gave preliminary approval, the Rouse plan would soon become a political football.

Jane Byrne included Navy Pier redevelopment as part of her plan for transforming Chicago into a world-class city, but plans alone could not win her re-election. In April 1983, Harold Washington succeeded Jane Byrne to become Chicago's first African-American chief executive.

Like his predecessors, Harold Washington appreciated Navy Pier, so much so he staged his inaugural there. Washington, however, defined priorities differently from Chicago's

ChicagoFest, held 1978 to 1982, further re-established Navy Pier as a center for entertainment and recreation. *Paul Natkin*

Harold Washington taking the oath of office at the pier auditorium, April 1983. The Washington administration favored developing the pier in a way different than that proposed by the Rouse Company. *Brett Jones*

57

earlier mayors who had focused their attention on downtown projects. Washington pursued a development strategy that linked the central business district to the neighborhoods; a project in one had to benefit the other. With Navy Pier, that connection was not so obvious.

Further, Washington was a political reformer determined to shake up city hall. Such a philosophy did not sit well with regular Democrats, who were in control of the city council. The ensuing struggle for power led to the so-called Council Wars. Day in and day out, the mayor and his opponents argued over the merits of one another's programs. This was the environment in which the Rouse plan now found itself.

A city-council committee dominated by the mayor's critics voted in February 1984 to end lease negotiations with Rouse; aldermen probably feared giving the mayor a political victory and control over a large development project. Conversely, the mayor may have been just as happy with the rejection of a proposal that did not reflect his own views. Washington then appointed a task force to propose a new plan for the pier's redevelopment.

The group reported back that it "enthusiasti-cally recommends the development of the Pier as an urban park with extensive and innovative cultural, educational and community activities." Included in this mix was the recommendation of only "limited retail activities." The pier would serve both as a traditional park and year-round recreational center. Also, "the task force envisions the pier as a community center whose base would be the entire city of Chicago. Its programs and facilities would both serve and reflect Chicago's diverse cultural life."

Similar proposals existed at the time for making the pier into a state or national park (an idea the National Park Service rejected in 1985). The various plans shared the idea of the pier as a place for largely passive recreation. This was the view that guided American park design throughout the nineteenth and into the early twentieth centuries. Central Park, Grant Park, Navy Pier: These were places intended to provide a sense of repose and an escape, however temporary, from city life.

There was an undeniable appeal in having Navy Pier conform to this ideal as a public forum. But American cities had undergone a fundamental change since Frederick Law

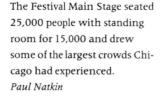

The Festival Main Stage seated 25,000 people with standing room for 15,000 and drew some of the largest crowds Chicago had experienced.
Paul Natkin

Olmsted designed parks for New York and Chicago. Cities no longer generated the wealth that once allowed them to build great parks or municipal piers. Navy Pier did not need to make money in the 1920s because Chicago possessed the tax base to make up the deficit. The 1980s were a different and far less prosperous world.

As cities scrambled to find ways to generate tax revenue, they invariably settled on tourism as a partial solution. It was a strategy that did not guarantee success. For every profitable Faneuil Hall there was a failure such as the world's fair in New Orleans (1984). Regardless of the possibility of failure, an increasing number of American cities felt the need to take the risk.

Any alternative Chicago was poised to take on Navy Pier ended with Harold Washington's sudden death in November 1987. Substantive action on the pier would be another two years off. Although new mayor Eugene Sawyer spent much of his time dealing with the city's unsettled political conditions, he was able to create the Navy Pier Development Authority in December 1988. The new authority and city hall then asked the Urban Land Institute to send an advisory panel to Chicago to develop recommendations for the pier's future.

The panel presented their findings in May 1989. They included a mix of public/private and commercial/noncommercial uses. Perhaps the most notable suggestion was for a city/state master-development authority be created to undertake the redevelopment of Navy Pier. Just as important for the pier was the mayoral election of Richard M. Daley a month earlier.

This Daley was no stranger to Navy Pier. As a boy, he had accompanied his father and brother William on their trip to the International Trade Fair in the summer of 1959. And like his father, the new mayor believed that economic growth depended in part on large development projects. With the decade's political tumult coming to an end, Navy Pier had a friend in city hall who was ready to act.

The pier also benefited from a friend in the governor's mansion. Not only was James R. Thompson a Chicagoan, he was an alum of the University of Illinois' Navy Pier campus. In office, Thompson proved an aggressive advocate of projects to diversify and thereby strengthen the state economy. Key to Thompson's strategy was Build Illinois, a special bond program for infrastructure work. Thompson agreed that Navy Pier was a project deserving of state support.

In 1989 the city and state agreed to dissolve

the authority in charge of McCormick Place and replace it with the Metropolitan Pier and Exposition Authority (MPEA), an independent municipal corporation with a board composed of state and city appointees. The authority would run both the pier and McCormick Place; as part of the agreement, the city sold Navy Pier to the MPEA for $10. The state also provided a $150 million Build Illinois grant for the pier. That December, the authority reviewed ten architectural proposals from twelve fully qualified participants.

"This is the Navy Pier bakeoff, and we're all peddling our latest cake," one of the participants joked. There was indeed a sense of the confectioner's art about some of the proposals. Designs included a performing arts center in the shape of a golden egg; a series of masts down the center of the pier with buildings grouped to resemble two massive ships' hulls; and a trellis of steel-framing down the length of the pier. Charles Frost might not have recognized his own creation.

The new pier authority chose a team of two architectural firms: VOA Associates, Inc., of Chicago and Benjamin Thompson and Associates, Inc., of Cambridge, Massachusetts. The VOA firm, who were the managing architects, had extensive experience in convention- and hospitality-related projects. The Thompson firm was widely recognized for their design of "people places" such as Faneuil Hall Quincy Market in Boston and for waterfront developments such as Baltimore's Harborplace. It was the hope of all those involved that the same kind of success would be repeated in Chicago.

And so Navy Pier, built in 1916 "for the people," stood ready for its first real makeover in seventy-five years. Everything old was about to become new again.

Jon Clay, Navy Pier general manager, James Reilly, Metropolitan Pier and Exposition Authority CEO, and Jerome Butler, deputy general manager of the pier in front of the historic east-end buildings. *Chicago Tribune photo by Bill Hogan*

MJ'S NUMBER BANNED

NBA Issues Fine, Says He Can't Wear No. 23 in Playoffs **Sports, Pages 137-139**

Chicago Sun-Times

35¢

Chicago/Suburbs
50¢ Elsewhere

BEAUTIFUL Pages 2, 57   FRIDAY, MAY 12, 1995   **Late Sports Final**

Nichols Had Bomb Material, Feds Say

Witnesses Spotted Truck at His Home

BY RICHARD A. SERRANO
and RONALD J. OSTROW
LOS ANGELES TIMES

EL RENO, Okla.—In the four days before the bombing of the federal building in Oklahoma City, Terry L. Nichols purchased large amounts of diesel fuel oil, and his neighbors reported seeing a large Ryder rental truck at his home and at a storage bin nearby, a federal affidavit said Thursday.

The affidavit, alleging Nichols' involvement in the worst terrorist attack in U.S. history, also asserts that the Ryder truck and a pickup truck matching one owned by Nichols, 40, were spotted on the morning before the April 19 bombing at a fishing lake not far from Nichols' home in Herington, Kan. Officials said they believe the fuel oil and large amounts of ammonium nitrate fertilizer were mixed together at the lake, then transported in the Ryder truck to Oklahoma City.

To bolster their claim that Nichols is a bomb expert and the brains behind assembling the deadly mixture, the affidavit said federal agents recovered blasting caps, bomb cords, a fuel meter and "several containers of ground ammonium nitrate" in a search of his home after he voluntarily surrendered in the case three weeks ago.

At Nichols' home, agents also seized guns, four white barrels with blue lids made from material **Turn to Page 22**

THE NEW NAVY PIER

RICH CHAPMAN/SUN-TIMES VIA SHADOW TRAFFIC HELICOPTER
The pier will have a Ferris wheel, concerts, restaurants and a beautiful view of Chicago.

After 79 years of glory and neglect, the pier is being transformed into a modern entertainment center, to be launched in the coming months

Special Report on Pages 6-7

INSIDE: Diagram Of the Changes

Rockefeller Center Bankrupt **Page 45**

Win $1,000 in 'Spot Check' **Page 36**

Denzel Washington

Ebert Reviews 7 Films, Including 'Crimson Tide'

WeekendPlus

A Second Golden Age

6

The rebuilt Navy Pier is at once familiar and new. While visitors may recognize the general outline of the pier, they will be amazed by all the rest—a children's museum, an outdoor stage, retail shops, restaurants, and more. Perhaps the most surprising change involves the calendar: The pier is no longer a summer-only destination. January might as well be June as people sit among the palm trees and fountains in the Crystal Gardens or as they stroll among the shops of the Family Pavilion. This transformation—along with the decision to keep admission free—has made Navy Pier a center of public activity along the lakefront, just as Daniel Burnham wanted nearly a century ago.

The new Navy Pier bears the imprint of two Metropolitan Pier and Exposition Authority (MPEA) officials in particular. John B. Schmidt was Mayor Richard M. Daley's choice to be the authority's first chairman; Jim Reilly was appointed authority CEO by Governor Jim Thompson. Schmidt and Reilly saw the pier as more than a generic tourist attraction. At their insistence, the planning staff explored ways of making Navy Pier a vibrant entertainment, recreation, and cultural facility that would attract a mass audience. At the same time, they understood that the pier had to generate revenue year-round or risk being labeled a failure. Kelly Welsh, who in June 1993 followed Schmidt as MPEA chairman, continued his predecessor's approach to the project.

Schmidt and Reilly directed the MPEA staff throughout the planning stages to pursue ideas for making the pier both unique and popular, and they oversaw the design studies that outlined the pier's modernization. Their combined efforts paid immediate dividends on the $200 million project. When the pier celebrated its rededication on July 12, 1995, the public left no doubt that it liked what John Schmidt and Jim Reilly worked to make possible.

The actual planning work dates to February 1991, when the MPEA approved a conceptual plan for developing the pier as a "public activity center." The pier would combine spaces and uses that would include pedestrian walkways;

open areas for simple enjoyment of the pier and lakefront; museum and exhibition space; retail and food offerings; and a winter garden. In addition, excursion boats would dock on the pier's south side, just as they had in the 1920s. The *Chicago Evening Post* had praised the pier in 1918 for its "beauty of situation and holiday attraction." The MPEA hoped to earn similar accolades for the refurbished Navy Pier.

Visitors today thus share many of the experiences that people enjoyed during the pier's first golden age. And again, the pier's least-noticed aspect may be the most important: Navy Pier has survived the test of time because of sound engineering. In large part, the MPEA benefited from the work of Edward Shankland, the chief engineer of the Harbor and Subway Commission and the official responsible for the pier's original engineering design. Engineers for the pier authority strengthened or replaced existing structural supports, added caissons, and updated utilities to modern standards. The result is a year-round pier ready to withstand the forces of nature.

Along the way to the 1995 rededication, the MPEA undertook one of the most extensive comprehensive planning exercises in recent years. The result of this process was the production of the Navy Pier/Turning Basin Guidelines by the city's Department of Planning. These addressed such issues as land use, transportation, activities, and aesthetics. The guidelines helped shape the Navy Pier plan.

The MPEA had a working model for pier redevelopment that outlined basic objectives, proposed uses, and design guidelines. To insure broad-based public participation and a quick start on pier redevelopment, the MPEA hired a number of consultants, including the planning firm of Trkla, Petigrew, Allen and Payne, Inc., and Jerome Butler, the former city architect and commissioner of public works who brought extensive knowledge of the pier to the project.

Butler along with Trkla, Petigrew, Allen and Payne worked to develop the Navy Pier concept plan with input from public agencies and citizens' groups. They also coordinated the efforts

MPEA Chairman John B. Schmidt and CEO Jim Reilly. *MPEA*

The Murphy/Jahn vision (*above*) featured a continuous steel framework, while the Lohan design team proposal incorporated a dramatic roof design and marina. *Richard Brinner, Fish Photography*

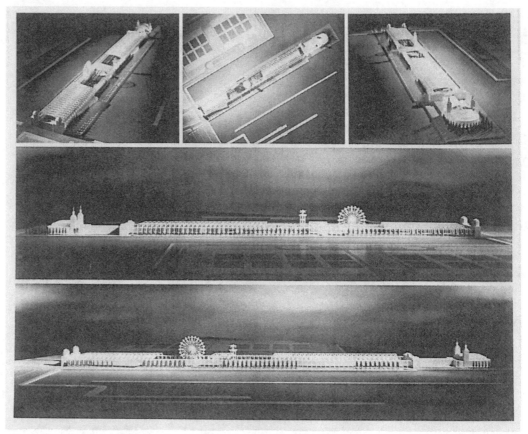

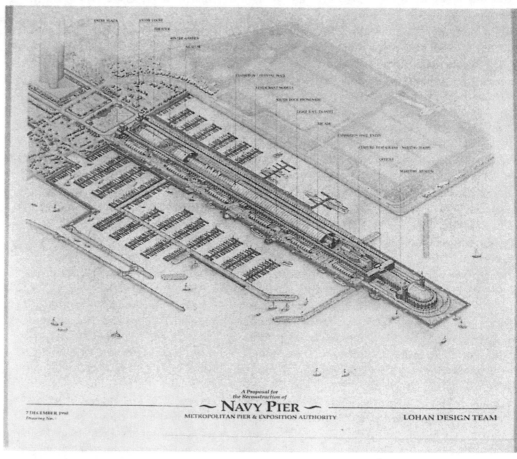

The Booth/Hansen vision of
Navy Pier at night. Note the
dramatic lighting effects.
Booth Hansen & Associates

of other consultants and worked with a group
of prominent Chicago architects who tested the
feasibility of the concept plan. The architects
developed their own versions of the redeveloped pier by incorporating all the proposed uses
and guidelines. The testing led to several signifi-
cant modifications. In addition, the MPEA hired
Jon Clay, an architect who had extensive experience with large projects, as director of development. Clay oversaw the design and construction
activities for the pier's redevelopment.

The project architects were selected through
a public process that permitted all qualified
firms to be considered for the project. A request
for qualifications was issued, and twenty-eight
firms or teams answered. The twelve found to
be fully qualified then were invited to submit
proposals. Ten responded.

Each respondent was evaluated by the crite-
ria outlined in the request for proposals. The
experience of participants was considered along
with their technical and financial qualifications.
What mattered most, however, was the designer's vision for the redeveloped pier and the
participant's success or track record on similar
projects.

The board was attracted to four ideas in particular. These were submitted by Booth Hanson,
RTKL Associates; Lohan Associates; Murphy/

Jahn Architects; and a team comprising VOA
Associates, Inc., and Benjamin Thompson and
Associates, Inc. Although all of the concepts
retained the original head house and east end
buildings (which had been designated city landmarks), there was considerable variation in the
way each architect approached the project.

The Booth Hanson/RTKL vision was entitled
"The Chicago Exposition at Navy Pier" and was
intended to recreate a Chicago heritage that
traced its roots to the Burnham Plan as well as
to the expositions of 1893 and 1933. The
scheme included new structures that recalled
the trusses and the industrial character of the
pier's original freight and passenger sheds.

Lohan Associates' proposal suggested new
structures that would be compatible with the
remaining historic buildings on the pier. The
new buildings, clad in masonry and glass, featured a dramatic roof design of arched, exposed
steel; the idea was to recall the copper-clad roof
of the pier's grand ballroom. This concept also
included a continuous linear building reminiscent of the original pier design.

The Murphy/Jahn vision offered a complete
departure from the architecture of the
remaining buildings. There was to be a continuous framework of steel columns and beams
supporting arched steel trusses; the framework

would span the pier and frame the enclosed, covered and open spaces designed beneath. While differing from the others, this bold concept also suggested a continuous silhouette and an industrial character reminiscent of the original pier.

The VOA/Benjamin Thompson proposal took a different tack. Rather than submit a concept that offered a clearly defined architectural expression, the team submitted a plan that illustrated the various uses and activities that would take place on the pier. Images from other "people places" created by the team were submitted along with a model of the pier to illustrate the "spirit" of the new Navy Pier. The architecture was intended to serve as a backdrop for the activities of people using the pier, in keeping with the design philosophy of Benjamin Thompson. The MPEA decided on this approach.

Ground breaking for the renovation work took place in August 1992. Among the dignitaries on hand was Governor Jim Edgar, who succeeded James Thompson in 1991. Edgar's presence served as more than a photo opportunity. It signaled the continuity of support for the project in Springfield. Despite an oftentimes contentious relationship between Chicago and downstate, Edgar continued his predecessor's refusal to let partisan politics interfere with Navy Pier funding.

The pier that opened in 1916 mixed the ideas of the Chicago Harbor and Subway Commission with those of Daniel Burnham. The commission intended the pier as part of an effort to make Chicago into one of the world's great ports. Burnham, however, wanted to reserve as much of the lakefront as possible for public use. Now with redevelopment, Navy Pier finally moves closer in spirit to the facility outlined in the Chicago Plan.

The pier acknowledges its civic role beginning at Jane Addams Park, located at Ohio Street and the lake. Here the Chicago Park District has renamed a four-acre park in honor of the founder of Hull House and recipient of the Nobel Peace Prize. The centerpiece of the park is a sculpture by Louise Bourgeois depicting a series of hands that Bourgeois has said represent "a plea for friendship, of kindness, compassion [and] tolerance because Jane Addams had this as an ideal."

Just to the south of the Addams Park sculpture (and southwest of the pier) is Du Sable Park, named for the city's first permanent resident, who lived nearby. When a statue honoring Jean Baptiste Point du Sable is erected, Chicago will have fashioned another important civic statement, that the city is the product of its du Sables and Burnhams, its masses and classes. All have helped to shape the history of Chicago, just as all are welcome to the new Navy Pier.

Also included as part of the pier's formal entrance is the nineteen-acre Gateway Park, constructed with the assistance of a $3.65 mil-

Getting started: MPEA CEO Jim Reilly cradles his hard hat as the rebuilding of Navy Pier begins, August 1992. To his right is Governor Jim Edgar; Mayor Richard M. Daley is standing between the two workmen. *MPEA*

lion grant from the National Park Service; funding was made possible through the support of U.S. Representative Sidney Yates of Chicago. The siting of the park offers a view of the pier in all of its rebuilt glory. The park is a far cry from the gravel parking lots and Quonset huts that once dominated the area.

A key element of Gateway Park is the computerized fountain built in black granite. The fountain is intended to be a landmark that shows just how various Navy Pier can be. The square-shaped design is the work of WET Design, which has completed similar projects for Walt Disney's Epcot Center. The Gateway Park fountain incorporates three series of jets, numbering 240 in all, that send water up to two hundred feet in the air. The fountain is, in a sense, a water sculpture that changes in outline, depending on the particular program being run. Unlike more formal designs, the Gateway fountain encourages people to play in it; with some of the jets at ground level, a per-son can simply stick out a hand or run across the pavement. Nighttime illumination adds yet another feature to the fountain.

Gateway Park serves a double purpose, as an entry to the pier and as a reminder of the role that Illinois's waterways have played in the region's history. A unique community art project emphasizes the latter. Funding for the park came about through the efforts of the Canal Corridor Association, which in 1984 helped convince Congress to recognize the old Illinois and Michigan Canal as a National Heritage Corridor.

The association later approached the Chicago Public Art Group, a local community-arts organization, to create an artwork celebrating the Heritage Corridor. The MPEA agreed that the area around Navy Pier and the mouth of the Chicago River made the perfect site for a project commemorating the way in which the water network has shaped the Chicago region's history.

The Gateway Fountain uses a
computer program to vary
the size of its water streams.
With some of the water jets
at street level, passersby have
the option of cooling off in
the summer heat. *Jerome
Butler*

Further discussion led to a plan consisting of three sculptural bench areas and a 1,300-foot, Y-shaped walkway representing the regional inland waterways: the Chicago River, Sanitary and Ship Canal, Illinois and Michigan Canal, Cal Sag Canal, and Illinois River. The plan also called for project artists to visit four Heritage Corridor communities, including the Chicago neighborhood of Bridgeport, to involve local artists and residents in the design of glass mosaics for the benches.

People arriving by automobile or taxi pass through Gateway Park to the North Dock. This is a fifty-foot-wide expansion of the pier along nearly its entire length which accommodates three traffic lanes together with a pedestrian walkway. Charter buses, automobiles, and delivery vehicles use this side of the pier, leaving the pier's south side, or "Dock Street," for pedestrians. The North Dock also provides access to the two enclosed parking garages located beneath the new pier construction. The garages offer a total of 1,150 spaces.

Visitors to Navy Pier encounter a facility that incorporates many of the elements of Charles

Frost's original design. The brick head house at the west end entrance together with the terminal and shelter buildings and the grand ballroom at the east end have all been restored to underscore their historic importance. However, the passenger and freight sheds—where university students roller-skated to class and tried to sneak into trade shows—are no more; the sheds proved too difficult to renovate and reuse. But in their place are structures similar in scope.

Dock Street recreates a sense of the past with a series of indoor walkways that resemble the south half of the old sheds. The construction was done in red brick together with extensive glass-and-steel framing. The brick of these new "sheds" matches the pier's original buildings, while the glass and steel figuratively connect the pier to the skyline of downtown.

The western portion of the walkway is fitted with glass doors, which makes the area an extension of Dock Street from spring through autumn. In the winter, with the vendors' carts inside, the walkway is transformed into an indoor market for piergoers who can choose from among the crafts, produce, and other mer-

Like a jigsaw puzzle in a million pieces: In late 1994, steel framing for Festival Hall stood ready to be assembled. *Richard Brinner, Fish Photography*

The rebuilding of Navy Pier included work on the foundation and the updating of utilities, including sewers. In the background is Lake Point Tower. *Richard Brinner, Fish Photography*

Steel framing going up in Festival Hall, early 1995. The hall is designed to attract mid-size conventions and trade shows that would find McCormick Place too large for their needs. *Richard Brinner, Fish Photography*

The rebuilt Navy Pier com-
bines new and old elements
in its design. Additional brick-
work was executed to comple-
ment that of the original
structures that were saved
and renovated by the MPEA.
MPEA

To accommodate vehicular traffic, the north side of the pier was widened by fifty feet. *Richard Brinner, Fish Photography*

chandise available. Further east, the walkway becomes a temperature-controlled passageway connecting the new activity areas.

Stretching 2,400 feet into Lake Michigan, Dock Street has become the heart and soul of the new Navy Pier. Signal flags, bollards, and chains recall the pier's nautical past, as does an eight-ton anchor from the USS *Chicago*, a heavy cruiser built during World War II. Dedicated on Veterans Day 1995, the anchor is a reminder of those who served in the war and, especially, those who trained on the pier.

The decorative street lamps along Dock Street are another reminder of the pier's history; their classic design recalls the time when Chicagoans first enjoyed the pleasures of their municipal pier. And, just as in the 1920s, the pier welcomes people who want nothing more than to stroll or fish within sight of downtown Chicago. Of course, walking is not the only way to experience Navy Pier. On less crowded days, roller bladers and cyclists also have been encouraged to discover the pier.

If they want, visitors to Dock Street can take advantage of the cruise ships moored alongside, as 600,000 people did during the pier's first summer of operation. They can also enjoy free entertainment at one of the four outdoor stages—or have it come to them in such unexpected form as a stilt walker or a cappella singing group. Piergoers can even find a bench, sit down, and take in what is without doubt the most striking panorama of the Chicago skyline.

The head house on the pier's west end has

Framing for the Skyline Stage (*far left*) resembled an insect caught in a snowstorm. Workmen are shown here attaching a fabric roof designed to withstand gale-force winds. *MPEA*

Fourteen months before the pier's rededication, foundation work was largely completed, and the Skyline Stage was ready to debut. *Richard Brinner, Fish Photography*

Opening ceremonies of July 12, 1995. Among those standing in the front row are (*from left*) MPEA CEO Jim Reilly; former governor Jim Thompson; Governor Jim Edgar; Secretary of the Navy John Dalton; Mayor Richard M. Daley; current MPEA chairman Kelly Welsh; and the Rev. John J. Wall. *MPEA*

This eight-ton anchor comes from the heavy cruiser USS *Chicago,* which saw service from the end of World War II to its decommissioning in 1980. The anchor has become a favorite spot for people to be photographed. *Wilmont Vickrey*

Entertainment comes in various shapes at Navy Pier, from unicycles and bikes to the 148-foot-tall Ferris wheel.

Seeing the big picture: Among those celebrating the opening of the 440-seat IMAX theater are (*second from left*) Ken Howarth of IMAX Corporation; Kelly R. Welsh, MPEA chairman; Keith Mallick, assistant general manager of entertainment at Navy Pier; and Jim Reilly, CEO of the MPEA. (*opposite top left*) MPEA

been renovated to welcome a new generation of pier visitors. Connected to it is the Family Pavilion, which contains forty thousand square feet of restaurant and retail space. This space is the focus of the year-round activity that has made Navy Pier so popular.

The use of the Family Pavilion is not bound by weather the way Navy Pier once was. Whereas winter used to restrict public activity on the pier, it now is the season marked by

carolers and a forty-eight-foot indoor Christmas tree. Whatever the time of year, the pavilion is Dock Street indoors, complete with vendors and entertainment. The shops offer a variety of goods, including jewelry, children's and adults' clothes, books, games, and souvenirs. Of particular interest is the Illinois Market Place, which features the museums, keepsakes, artistry, and history of the state. A collaborative effort on the part of city and state government, the store

offers a video tour of the state along with information on points of interest throughout metropolitan Chicago and Illinois.

And, if the mood strikes, visitors can avail themselves of the pavilion's restaurants. A McDonald's is designed around the theme of outer space, so fast food comes with a futuristic twist. There are also a food court and more formal dining establishments that allow patrons to take advantage both of the food and the scenery.

The Family Pavilion also is home to the Chicago Children's Museum. The museum continues the pier's tradition of serving children. Based on the idea that children often learn best by doing, the museum offers interactive workshops, special events, and school programs. The combination of site and program makes for a singular opportunity, as noted by museum executive director Dianne Sautter: "The lake, the open spaces, the [surrounding] gardens and parks all offer endless possibilities for the museum to ignite in children a love of exploration and learning." In addition, the museum's children's store features items to challenge youthful imaginations.

Among the other spaces in the Family Pavilion is the 440-seat IMAX Theater with 3-D capability. The theater screen measures six stories tall, or sixty by eighty feet. A special seventy-millimeter projector—weighing one ton—comes with a state-of-the-art sound system. In effect the theater creates a real-life experience for the audience. Thanks to IMAX, going to the show will never be the same.

Another pleasing addition to the pier is the

33,000-square-foot Crystal Gardens, framed in glass and steel. The gardens are suggestive of Joseph Paxton's design for the Crystal Palace, part of the London International Exhibition of 1851. Paxton demonstrated that space created by structures of glass with metal framing could be both practical and beautiful. The English writer Patrick Beaver recalled his visits as a schoolboy. The grounds were crowned by "the translucent mass that was the Crystal Palace and in the rays of the sun it was a mountain of light. I never tired of the place." Visitors to the Crystal Gardens will have much the same reaction.

The gardens also draw on the tradition of Chicago's two great conservatories in Lincoln

One reason for the pier's immediate success are restaurants that combine scenery and menu into an outstanding dining experience. *Lyal Lauth*

Located in the Family Pavilion, the Chicago Children's Museum teaches its youthful visitors the value of water as a resource and, as one exhibit explains, the Stinking Truth about Garbage. *Steve Kagan*

The Crystal Gardens continue a Chicago tradition of providing a green environment regardless of the weather outside. The gardens allow a family to relax or eat a quick meal among palm trees and fountains, no small pleasure come winter. *MPEA*

The Family Pavilion and Crystal Gardens are among the attractions that draw visitors to Navy Pier throughout the year. A year-round calendar of events keeps the pier busy. *MPEA*

Vendors at the Family Pavilion help create a marketplace atmosphere where a surprise gift may be just around the corner. *Avis Mandel*

and Garfield Parks. In Chicago's climatic zone, winter can reign both long and hard. But the glass-and-metal conservatories create spaces that house lush environments regardless of the weather. The Crystal Gardens do the same—the clusters of palm trees and fountains standing within sight of a shoreline frozen over with ice by January. People can sit and relax or experience the sensation of standing under a "trellis" formed by streams of shooting water. The gardens also look out on a reflecting pool that becomes a skating rink come winter. Whatever

Cold weather no longer means an end to activity on the pier, as these skaters prove to onlookers. *MPEA*

77

The two thousand-foot length of Dock Street draws visitors with its array of food, entertainment, and vendors. Classic street lamps and nautical touches recall the pier's past, while free admission invites the curious to explore all the changes that have taken place at the pier. *Avis Mandel*

The $400,000 musical carousel at Navy Pier features thirty-six custom-made menagerie animals. In addition, scenes from the pier's history are incorporated into the carousel's canopy. *MPEA*

the season, the view from the gardens is impressive.

East of the Family Pavilion and Crystal Gardens is the open-air Skyline Stage. When it debuted in May 1994, Skyline Stage immediately became one of the most pleasing entertainment stages in the Chicago region. No other performance pavilion is located directly on the Chicago lakefront, and surely no stage resembles this one. With steel framing reaching up seventy-five feet covered by a roof of white Teflon-coated fiberglass, Skyline Stage has already become a prominent feature for miles along the shores of Lake Michigan.

The fabric roof weighs some two tons and has a life expectancy of twenty-five years. It is fitted over a framework of steel tubing and is kept in place by steel cables connected to columns outside the tent. The framing is designed to withstand the rigors of Chicago's weather.

Architecture critic Blair Kamin of the *Tribune* described Skyline Stage as a "lighter-than-air

stagehouse" for the effect the design has on audiences. Those sitting in the 1,500-seat theater experience the entertainment on stage, and more. The open sides of Skyline stage make it as much an outdoor as an indoor venue. The sails of passing boats, the lake breeze, the sun illuminating the skyline—these serve as a backdrop for performances that range from the classical to popular. With floors warmed by a radiant heat system, the stage can extend its season early into spring and late into autumn.

Two amusement rides just east of the Crystal Gardens are also firmly rooted in Chicago history. Children who visited the pier in the 1920s had the opportunity to ride a carousel, and so do those who come now. A musical carousel designed exclusively for the pier features thirty-six custom-made menagerie animals. Parent and child can choose from horse, sea dragon, lion, and rabbit, among others. The carousel's canopy includes scenes from the pier's history.

And then there is the Ferris wheel. At 148 feet tall and 600 tons heavy and with the capacity to carry 240 people, this ride invites comparisons to the 264-foot-tall original that served fairgoers at the Columbian Exposition. Each of the forty gondolas on the new ride has room for six passengers. The ride rests on a 200,000-pound base and turns on a 17,000-pound axle. Eight electric motors move the wheel. In case of emergency, the wheel is so perfectly balanced that it can be turned on a winch.

The seven-and-a-half minute ride allows people to sightsee up and down the lakefront as an audio history and city travelogue points out landmarks past and present. At night, the wheel becomes a great light sculpture with illumination on both sides provided by sixteen thousand light bulbs. The Ferris wheel operates from May through October.

The rides form part of the backdrop for Festival Hall, which fills an important role in the Chicago trade and convention industry. The 170,000-square-foot exhibition hall is meant to accommodate shows that are too big for hotels

People are not alone in
enjoying events staged in Festival Hall. *Lyal Lauth*

The excusion boats that line Dock Street are reminiscent of Navy Pier in the 1920s. *MPEA*

A big band plays to the delight of the audience in the grand ballroom during opening-week festivities at the pier. *James Steinkamp, Steinkamp Associates*

and yet too small for Chicago's giant McCormick Place. Festival Hall is also home to such annual events as flower and art shows. Whatever the event, Festival Hall returns Navy Pier to its former use as a trade and convention center. And now exhibitors get a modern space to go with the beautiful location.

The Grand Ballroom on the pier's east end has been completely renovated to appear as it did in 1916, as one of the most breathtaking spaces in all Chicago for parties and concerts. Among the ballroom's most striking features are an eighty-foot-high ceiling outlined in tivoli lights, the second-floor balcony, and a 180-degree view of Lake Michigan; these combine to offer the perfect setting for any event. With its direct connection to Festival Hall, the auditorium can function as an additional facility for shows and conventions taking place there.

While the rebuilt Navy Pier cannot help but draw attention, the MPEA has not left the pier's popularity to chance. Instead, the authority has used an extensive schedule of events to build and maintain interest. Film festivals, concerts, a haunted house for Halloween, Santa Claus in the Crystal Gardens—these are some of the

offerings that introduce people to the new Navy Pier. Visitors may come for a single event or a trade show, but they will likely come back because of what they saw.

Some are drawn to those aspects of the pier reminiscent of its first golden age nearly eighty years ago. People who want to relive the pier's past can do so by seeing a movie, having dinner, or taking a cruise. They can use the pier as a place to take children or a place for fishing, both at little or no cost. Visitors also can listen to music at the pier's outdoor beer garden, and this time drinking will not draw the attention of Prohibition agents. Visitors will even find that Navy Pier is again home to a radio station with a sense of mission; WBEZ, the local outlet for National Public Radio, has relocated to the pier. So much of what is new, down to the carousel, has its roots in the original Navy Pier.

Or, if the attraction is the state-of-the-art recreation, entertainment, and convention center, visitors to Navy Pier can sample everything that is truly new: the finer restaurants, Skyline Stage, IMAX Theater, retail shops, and Crystal Gardens. Either way, the new Navy Pier has become a facility to match the various moods of its users for education, recreation, or entertainment. All a person has to do is decide.

Probably the only elements of the pier's past missing today are naval recruits and university students rushing to class. But who knows what the future will bring in this second golden age? Just about anything is possible at Navy Pier.

MANUSCRIPT COLLECTIONS

Chicago Historical Society.

Municipal Reference Collection, Harold Washington Public Library, Chicago.

Naval Historical Center, Washington, D.C.

Ryerson and Burnham Libraries, Art Institute of Chicago.

University of Illinois at Chicago Alumni Association.

University of Illinois at Chicago University Library University Collections.

Suggested Reading

A. T. Andreas. *History of Chicago from the Earliest Period to the Present Time*, 3 vols. Chicago, 1884.

Patrick Beaver. *The Crystal Palace, 1851–1936: A Portrait of Victorian Enterprise*. London, 1970.

Douglas Bukowski. "According to Image: Big Bill Thompson and Chicago Politics." Ph.D dissertation, University of Illinois at Chicago.

David F. Burg. *Chicago's White City of 1893*. Lexington, Ky., 1976.

Daniel H. Burnham and Edward H. Bennett. *The Chicago Plan*. New York, 1970.

Louis P. Cain. "The Creation of Chicago's Sanitary District and Construction of the Sanitary and Ship Canal." *Chicago History*, Summer 1979.

Carl W. Condit. *Chicago, 1910–1929: Building, Planning, and Urban Technology*. Chicago, 1973.

_____. *Chicago, 1930–1970: Building, Planning, and Urban Technology*. Chicago, 1974.

William Cronon. *Nature's Metropolis: Chicago and the Great West*. New York, 1991.

Emmett Dedmon. *Fabulous Chicago*. Chicago, 1981.

Perry R. Duis. *We've Got a Job to Do: Chicagoans and World War II*. Chicago, 1992.

Donald Drew Egbert. *The Beaux-Arts Tradition in French Architecture*. Princeton, N.J., 1980.

James L. Elliott. *Red Stacks over the Horizon: The Story of the Goodrich Steamship Line*. Grand Rapids, Mi., 1967.

James R. Grossman. *Land of Hope: Chicago, Black Southerners, and the Great Migration*. Chicago, 1989.

Thomas S. Hines. *Burnham of Chicago: Architect and Planner*. Chicago, 1979.

Susan E. Hirsch and Robert I. Goler. *A City Comes of Age: Chicago in the 1890s*. Chicago, 1990.

Glen E. Holt and Dominic A. Pacyga. *Chicago: A Historical Guide to the Neighborhoods, the Loop and South Side*. Chicago, 1979.

Bernard R. Kogan. "Chicago's Pier." *Chicago History*, Spring 1976.

Herman Kogan and Lloyd Wendt. *Big Bill of Chicago*. Indianapolis, 1953.

John Lamb. *Illinois and Michigan Canal: A Corridor in Time*. Romeoville, Il., 1986.

Lloyd Lewis and Henry Justin Smith. *Chicago: The History of its Reputation*. New York, 1929.

Harold M. Mayer and Richard C. Wade. *Chicago: Growth of a Metropolis*. Chicago, 1969.

Edward E. Nugent. "The Paddle Wheelers of the 1940s." *Foundation*, Spring 1994.

Bessie Louise Pierce. *A History of Chicago*, 3 vols. Chicago, 1975.

_____, ed. *As Others See Chicago: Impressions of Visitors, 1673–1933*. Chicago, 1933.

Robert A. Slayton. *Back of the Yards: The Making of a Local Democracy*. Chicago, 1986.

Lois Wille. *Forever Open, Clear and Free: The Struggle for Chicago's Lakefront*. Chicago, 1991.

Navy Pier has been a land-mark since its opening in 1916. The MPEA based its renovation plan on the pier's obvious strengths. Day or night, January or June, Navy Pier gives proof of Chicago's rise as a center for tourism. *Rose Sandura from David Maenza*

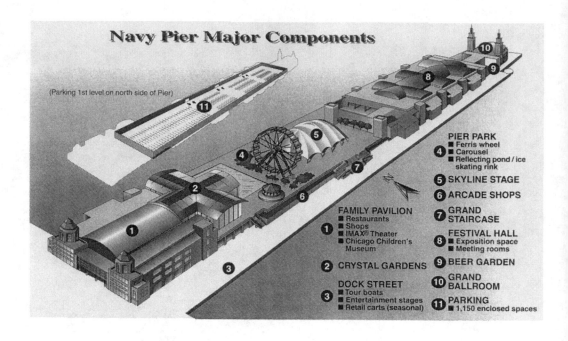

Navy Pier Major Components

(Parking 1st level on north side of Pier)

FAMILY PAVILION
① ■ Restaurants
   ■ Shops
   ■ IMAX® Theater
   ■ Chicago Children's
     Museum

② CRYSTAL GARDENS

DOCK STREET
③ ■ Tour boats
   ■ Entertainment stages
   ■ Retail carts (seasonal)

PIER PARK
④ ■ Ferris wheel
   ■ Carousel
   ■ Reflecting pond / ice
     skating rink

⑤ SKYLINE STAGE

⑥ ARCADE SHOPS

⑦ GRAND
  STAIRCASE

FESTIVAL HALL
⑧ ■ Exposition space
   ■ Meeting rooms

⑨ BEER GARDEN

⑩ GRAND
  BALLROOM

PARKING
⑪ ■ 1,150 enclosed spaces

Navy Pier fact sheet

Architects
1916: Charles Sumner Frost, Chicago, Illinois
1976: Jerome R. Butler, City Architect,
Chicago, Illinois
1995: VOA Associates, Chicago, Illinois

Children's Museum
Cost: $14.5 million
Size: 57,000 sq. ft. (three levels)
Visitors: 500,000+ per year
Major exhibits: Climbing Schooner, Inventing
  Lab, Waterways, Treehouse Trails, Play-
  Maze, Artabounds, and OnCamera

Cost of Pier
Original construction (total project):
$5 million (1916)
Reconstruction: $200 million (1995)

Cruise Boats
Four dinner cruise boats dock at Navy Pier
and serve more than 600,000 passengers per
year. In addition, the pier is home to a sight-
seeing boat, a four-masted schooner, *Windy*,
and a 150-passenger speedboat, *The Seadog*.

Crystal Gardens
Height: 60 ft.; Area: 33,000 sq. ft.; Glass surface: 45,000 sq. ft.
Special features
  • 71 Palm trees
  • 20 "Laminar flow" fountains
  • Fully air conditioned and heated

Ferris Wheel
Operating season: May–October
Height: 148 ft.; Weight: 600 tons; Gondolas:
40; Total capacity: 240 passengers; Cost: $3.2
million; Number of lights: 16,000; Revolution
time: 7.5 minutes

Festival Hall
Ceiling height: 60 ft.; Length: 810 ft.; Width:
210 ft.; Exhibit floor: 170,100 sq. ft.; Truck
docks: 10; Meeting rooms: 35
Types of Events: Flower and garden show,
  International art fair, antique shows, winter indoor inline skating, county fair, auto
  shows, boat show, basketball and tennis
  tournaments, computer shows, kennel
  show, miscellaneous trade shows

Gateway Fountain
Number of water jets: 240
Maximum water height: 200 ft.
Cost: $1 million

Gateway Park
Size: 19 acres
Key features
  • Gateway Fountain
  • 40 Decorative benches
  • 526 Trees

Grand Ballroom
Originally built: 1916; Renovated: 1976
Height: 60 ft. (domed ceiling); Area: 17,500
sq. ft.
Seating capacity
  • Theater: 2,000
  • Dinner: 1,500

IMAX Theater
440 Seats
Special features
  • 3-D
  • Surround sound
Cost: $4.5 million
Screen size
  • Width: 80 ft.
  • Height: 60 ft.

Key Dates
First opened: June 25, 1916
Reconstruction groundbreaking: August 25, 1992
Grand celebration: July 12, 1995

Lake Michigan
Surface area: 23,300 sq. miles; Deepest point: 923 ft.
Depth at pier
  • South Dock: 27 ft.
  • North Dock: 16 ft.

Location of Pier
600 East Grand Avenue
Chicago, Illinois 60611

Miscellaneous
Caissons: 900 (90 ft. to bedrock); Benches: 450; Bollards: 300; Decorative light poles: 205

Musical Carousel
Capacity: 50 (36 animals; 4 benches)
Cost: $400,000
Operating season: May–October

North Dock
Length: 2,300 ft.; Width: 50 ft.; Three traffic lanes; Pedestrian promenade with trees in planters

Parking Garages
Locations
  • East: Below Festival Hall
  • West: Below Pier Park
Indoor parking spaces: 1,150

Pier Dimensions
Length: 3,000 ft.; Width: 440 ft.

Radio Station
WBEZ Public Radio (91.5 FM)
Studios located at west end of Festival Hall
Transmits from John Hancock Building
300,000 listening audience weekly

Reflecting Pond
Size: 60 ft. × 100 ft.; Depth: 1 ft.; Water volume: 50,000 gallons; Five fountains
Special features
  • Converts to ice rink in winter
  • Radio-controlled miniature boats in summer

Restaurants
The pier is home to an outdoor beer garden, numerous seasonal concession stands, four year-round, full-service restaurants, the nation's largest theme McDonald's, and a diverse food court featuring Chinese food, deli items, pizza, hot dogs, and ice cream specialties.

Retailers
In addition to the Chicago Children's Museum and the Navy Pier IMAX 3D Theater, year-round tenants in the Family Pavilion include a magic shop, bookstore, game store, flags and banners store, city-state souvenir shop, children's wear store, toy store, and newsstand.

Seasonal Vendors
More than 50 seasonal concessionaires and vendors add excitement to the pier's Dock Street. These feature: hand-drawn caricatures; bike and inline skate rental; handcrafted and antique jewelry; ties; Native American, African American, and Hispanic fashions; wind chimes; hand-blown glass; popcorn; roasted peanuts; lemon ice; cotton candy; and hot dogs.

Skyline Stage
Seating capacity: 1,500; Structure: Teflon-coated fiberglass; Height: 75 ft.; Sound system: multipurpose, directional; Cost: $8.8 million; Season: May–October
Typical Events: Navy Pier Pops Orchestra, ethnic festivals, children's theater, jazz and blues fest, Chicago Symphony Orchestra, folk music, and ballet

South Arcade
Length: 850 ft.; Width: 30–45 ft.

South Dock
Length: 2,300 ft.; Width: 90 ft.
Special features
  • Grand staircase
  • Fishing and performance pavilions
  • Cart market

Visitors
3.5–4 million per year

Navy Pier Access Map

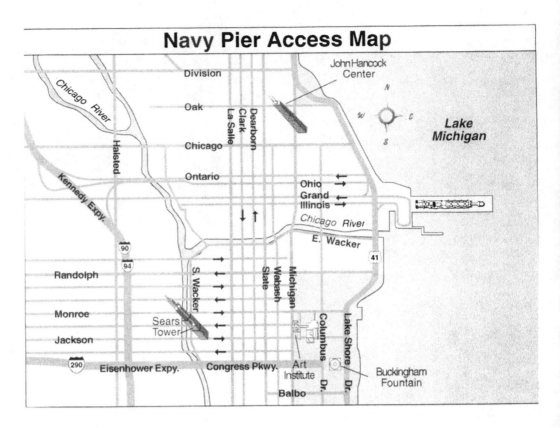

About the Author

Douglas Bukowski received his Ph.D. in American history at The University of Illinois, Chicago. He is the author of BASEBALL PALACE OF THE WORLD: THE LAST YEAR OF COMISKEY PARK (Lyceum Books, Inc.) and numerous articles on Chicago history and politics. Together with his wife, Michele, he fully expects their daughter, Clare, to break Pete Rose's all-time record for base hits.

Author's Acknowledgments

I wish to thank the staff of the Municipal Reference Collection of the Harold Washington Library for their ability to find any and all documents no matter how arcane and Jerry Butler and John Devona for sharing their knowledge of the pier as well as their enthusiasm for seeing this project through to completion.

A Note on Type

Meridien, designed by Adrian Frutiger in 1955, a classical typeface which shows the designer's feelings for the incised origins of roman lettering.

Book development and packaging:
Lyceum Books, Inc., Chicago, Illinois

Design: Cameron Poulter Design, Chicago, Illinois

Photo research: Carol Parden,
Image Resources, Inc., Chicago, Illinois

Typesetting: Precision Typographers, Inc., Michigan City, Indiana

Printing and Binding:
Freisens Corporation, Altona, Canada

Research and Writing Grant:
Graham Foundation for Advanced Studies in the Fine Arts

CPSIA information can be obtained at www.ICGtesting.com
Printed in the USA
BVOW07s1821290415

398057BV00002B/2/P